'I was rather worried before I read *How Not To Worry* that I may unearth some abnormality or imperfection about myself. I needn't have been concerned. I feel quite normal now. Paul's approach to this subject is fantastic. It's as though he's sat across from you having a chat. Extremely easy to read, very interesting and with some simple ideas of how to have a worry-less life. Highly recommended.'

Richard McCann, *Sunday Times* Number One Bestselling Author of *iCan* and Inspirational Speaker

'*How Not to Worry* is a down to earth book, which can help the many "walking wounded worriers" deal with the small stresses in life that create sleepless nights. It is well written and very practically orientated, and should help you confront and deal with the many stresses and strains that lead to worrying.'

Professor Cary Cooper, CBE, Distinguished Professor of Organizational Psychology and Health, Lancaster University

'We all need help in dealing with the pressures of modern living, whatever walk of life we're from. I recognize the pressures that come from high expectations and know that this book will provide you with both the insight and the inspiration to deal more effectively with the challenges of life. Paul McGee's approach is practical and honest as he shares his own personal experiences. A powerful read.'

Shay Given, Aston Villa and Republic of Ireland Goalkeeper

'Enlightening and engaging, you are bound to discover ideas and insights to help you deal with the pressures of life.'

Rosemary Conley, CBE

'If ever a book's subject was right for a point in time, it's this one. Businesses of today are worried – about the economy, cheap competitors, demanding customers, demotivated staff... the list is endless.

'But, if you can't fix your own oxygen mask, how can you even begin to think about helping others?

'This book provides simple, practical ways for you to help both yourself and others. To focus on the positives, not simply avoid the negatives. To thrive, not merely survive. A great guide to help you achieve a more sane and enjoyable life.'

Andy Bounds, Britain's Sales Trainer of the Year

'I'm not usually a great fan of this kind of book, but Paul McGee's approach is both enjoyable and useful. It could go a long way to help alleviate some of the unnecessary worries that people become trapped by. Don't just read it, but apply the ideas as well.'

Kevin Morley, Channel 4's *Secret Millionaire* and Former Managing Director of Rover Car Group

'This book will prove a valuable resource for people wishing to gain some understanding of managing a broad range of stressful emotions. Paul McGee manages to present the facets of this all too common trait in a clear no-nonsense digestible form that enables the reader to identify their own unique "triggers" and provides a tool kit of ideas and suggestions for coping with, dealing with and above all altering reactions. He provides plausible examples that give the reader practical guidelines to apply in "their world." Make it a permanent resident of your handiest reference shelf.'

Jean Donnell Jones, Cognitive Psychologist, Cheshire Counselling and Training Services

'I really didn't expect to get so much benefit from a book I didn't think I needed to read. I'd imagine this is invaluable for someone who believes they struggle with stress, anxiety or worry, but also for anyone else to help them get a better understanding so they may support someone who does! Quite often our ignorance to these issues stops people asking for support when they desperately need it. Well done Paul for producing an easy to digest book that will help people at all levels.'

Jamie Stewart, Managing Director of Kleeneze

'I hate this book. If my clients are not worried, they just won't need me. McGee's techniques are so annoyingly clever and frustratingly accessible that he might have just put the entire self-help and coaching industries out of business.'

Graham Davies, Author of *The Presentation Coach*

'A practical, realistic and effective approach to dealing with a serious topic. This book is an excellent and insightful read sprinkled with the occasional dash of humour. As you'll learn, achieving success doesn't mean worry and stress come with the territory. This book shows you how to enjoy the pressures of life rather than be weighed down by them.'

Kevin Gaskell, Former Managing Director of BMW, Porsche and Lamborghini and Successful Serial Entrepreneur

'This book is brilliant. Paul McGee speaks to you personally off the pages, and his advice is spot-on. He understands why we worry, and how we can stop doing it. If you've ever worried about anything, at any time, this is the book for you.'

Alan Stevens, The MediaCoach, Past President, Global Speakers Federation

'If you find that the epidemic of fear and worry that pervades the developed world affects you, then you need to read Paul McGee's wonderful book. Your life will be the richer – and quite possibly, longer – for it.'

Fergus O'Connell, bestselling author of *Simply Brilliant* and *Earn More, Stress Less*

How Not To Worry

How Not To Worry

The Remarkable Truth of How a Small
Change Can Help You Stress Less and
Enjoy Life More

Paul McGee

Illustrations by Fiona Griffiths

CAPSTONE

This edition first published 2012

© 2012 Paul McGee

Illustrations © Fiona Griffiths

Registered office
Capstone Publishing Ltd. (A Wiley Company), The Atrium, Southern Gate, Chichester, West Sussex, PO19 8SQ, United Kingdom.

For details of our global editorial offices, for customer services and for information about how to apply for permission to reuse the copyright material in this book please see our website at www.wiley.com.

Wiley publishes in a variety of print and electronic formats and by print-on-demand. Some material included with standard print versions of this book may not be included in e-books or in print-on-demand. If this book refers to media such as a CD or DVD that is not included in the version you purchased, you may download this material at http://booksupport.wiley.com. For more information about Wiley products, visit www.wiley.com.

Library of Congress Cataloging-in-Publication Data
McGee, Paul, 1964-
  How not to worry : The Remarkable Truth of How a Small Change Can Help You Stress Less and Enjoy Life More / Paul McGee ; illustrations by Fiona Griffiths.
  p. cm.
  Includes index.
  ISBN 978-0-85708-286-2
  1. Worry. 2. Anxiety. 3. Calmness. I. Title.
  BF575.W8M36 2012
  152.4'6--dc23
                                     2012007153

A catalogue record for this book is available from the British Library.

ISBN 978-0-857-08286-2 (pbk) ISBN 978-0-857-08292-3 (ebk)
ISBN 978-0-857-08294-7 (ebk) ISBN 978-0-857-08293-0 (ebk)

Set in 11/14 Baskerville by Sparks – www.sparkspublishing.com

Printed in Great Britain by TJ International Ltd, Padstow, Cornwall, UK

To H and Stinx with love

Contents

About Paul McGee   **xiii**

Introduction   **1**

SECTION ONE: Stop, Understand   **9**

1   The Big Deal About Worry   11
2   Why Do We Worry?   29
3   Are We Wired to Worry?   65
4   Ever Got Lost in Loopy Logic?   87

SECTION TWO: Move On   **115**

5   Let's Get Rational   117
6   Manage Your Imagination   145
7   Show a Little Respect... to Yourself   167
8   How to Make Your Environment Friendly   199

And Finally...   **221**
Further Reading   **229**
Index   **233**

About Paul McGee

Paul McGee is one of the UK's leading speakers on the areas of change, confidence, workplace relationships, motivation and stress. His thought-provoking, humorous and practical approach to life's challenges has seen him speak in 35 countries to date and he is the author of seven books. He is also a performance and life coach working with one of the English Premiership's leading football clubs.

The proud creator of S.U.M.O. (Shut Up, Move On), his simple yet profound messages have spread across the globe both in public and private sector organizations. More recently his ideas have been developed for young people under the banner of SUMO4Schools.

Building on his academic background in behavioural and social psychology, Paul is also a trained counsellor, a performance coach and a Fellow of the Professional Speaking Association.

His aim is simple – 'I want to help people achieve better results in life and have more fun in the process'.

For more information visit **www.TheSumoGuy.com** or follow Paul on Twitter: **@TheSumoGuy**

Introduction

I'm not sure what percentage of your family have to describe themselves as worriers for you to say you're from a family of worriers, but I must come pretty close.

That's not to be critical of my family. Not all of them fit into that category, and indeed my own father would be at the complete opposite end of the spectrum. But I do come close.

So I guess it's fair to say this topic is particularly near to my heart.

During the writing of this book when I mentioned to people the title, the majority instantly replied 'I'll be getting a copy of that when it comes out'.

Now if I'm honest I wasn't sure if that last statement was a command or a sign of real interest in the subject. Are they expecting me, the author, who has slaved over the manuscript for months, to send them a free copy (signed of course) or do they genuinely believe that they too, like many of my family, are worriers and could do with some help along the way?

I'm hoping it's the latter.

I need the royalties.

Hey, just kidding.

Seriously, I do hope that the subject matter does have wide appeal and wherever you place yourself on the worry spectrum you find ideas and insights that prove invaluable in dealing with what seems to be becoming an increasingly challenging problem.

As we'll see in our first chapter, people use a variety of terms to describe their worries and in fact the word 'worry' might not be one of them.

That's OK.

My belief is that few of us react to life's challenges in quite the way we'd like to and that whatever label we use to describe our response you'll find some good stuff cropping up amongst the following pages that will help you on your journey.

I've written a number of books that fall within the self help/ business category and I'm humbled when from time to time people describe reading one of them as life changing.

Some people are perhaps a little more subdued in their feedback but still usually make a few positive noises about what I've written.

And there are a few people who, it pains me to say, get very little if anything from reading my material.

Interestingly enough, though, I can get all the above responses from people who've all read the same book.

So I guess to some extent how you engage with what you're about to read depends on where you're currently at in life, and also why you've picked up this book in the first place. If you've decided on reading this to kill a few hours at an airport or because you fancied a read for your train journey you may approach the subject matter in a somewhat different way from the person who has felt plagued with worry throughout their lives and is looking for some help and inspiration.

Well, wherever you're at, here's what you can expect in terms of my style and approach:

The book has been divided into two sections. I've called the first section 'Stop, Understand'. I want to explore why worry seems to be such a big deal, what the reasons are for it and expose some of the behavioural traps we fall into when we're dealing with some of life's challenges.

My goal in doing to is to get you to take some time to reflect and also gain a greater understanding of the subject. You see, I want to explore the causes, not just the consequences, of worry.

That in turn should set us up nicely for the second section, which I've called 'Move On'. Having gained insights from the first half I then want to explore a range of practical tools and ideas to help us deal with our worries and challenges (real or otherwise) in a more constructive way. Even in this 'Move On' section I'll give you the opportunity for some reflection – and throughout the book you'll come across sections called 'Hammock Time' which will give you a chance to reflect on what you've just read. You may be tempted to skip over these in the belief that all you need to help you change is more information and taking time to pause and reflect only slows down that journey.

Wrong.

Big time.

You'll gain far more from reading this book if you take time to chew over some of the ideas and even complete some of the exercises.

Here's the deal.

I'm not promising a magic cure.

I'm not even prescribing a set of quick-fix solutions.

I am, however, saying if you take time to engage with what's been written you'll significantly increase the value you gain from reading it. Not only that but you'll discover strategies that won't only benefit you but you can also pass onto others.

Also be aware that in writing this book I did have a picture of the kind of person reading it.

You're probably female. Average height. Dark hair. In a relationship. And your star sign is Libra.

I'm joking. Although if you are all of the above then this is getting spooky isn't it?

What I mean is, I do have a general picture of the kind of person I'm writing this book for.

And without trying to undermine you in any way I'm thinking you're like the majority of people who would be drawn to read this kind of book.

Fairly normal.

I don't mean that to insult you. I just think that like me you probably sometimes find life a challenging juggling act and also a bit of a rollercoaster at times. However, you're not on the verge of mental meltdown and neither are you using this material as your main text for your PHD thesis on 'The societal effects of stress in the 21st century and its philosophical and economic implications'.

You may or may not have children, but if you do you'll probably relate to the quote that says 'Having children is a mixture of pure joy and guerrilla warfare'.

And the word 'struggle' would not be an accurate description to describe all aspects of your life but it may have crept onto your radar from time to time, particularly more recently.

You may, however, have been affected by the aftershock of the current economic climate and be more concerned about your future now than perhaps at any stage of your life so far. Or perhaps you're a little like my wife, who generally tends to be a laid-back kind of person but would still like to worry less about stuff than she does now.

If you can identify with some of the above, then welcome to how the vast majority of people are probably feeling at present. And if you don't fall into any of the above categories I'd be surprised if you don't know several people who do.

Now can I let you into a secret?

I do have a small confession to make.

Most of what I write is rather simple and straightforward. Strangely that can be a problem to some people.

In some ways they may feel cheated or robbed.

I guess complex intellectual answers do in some ways massage our egos. Simple ones don't.

However, let me be clear.

Simple does not mean easy.

I think the theory of losing weight seems quite simple. Eat less, exercise more.

Simple.

But not always easy.

Agree?

So let me assure you, I've worked really hard to make what I write simple and accessible. I hope you'll find that to be the case, and that simple has not crossed over into being overly simplistic. In fact I take some encouragement from the late Steve Jobs, who said 'Simple can be harder than complex. You have to work hard to get your thinking clear to make it simple. But it's worth it in the end because once you get there you can move mountains.' (*Business Week*, 25 May 1998.)

My goal is also to point out the obvious. Most things are obvious aren't they?

In hindsight.

Dotted throughout my writing will be some personal anecdotes. Suffering three close bereavements in four months, moving house and office on the same day, seeing my son leave home for the first time and experiencing complications after what was supposed to be a routine operation, all whilst writing this book, have certainly added experience as well as insight into what I'm about to share. And although some of those experiences have been difficult they've also kept me firmly rooted in the real world and a safe distance from ivory towers.

I'm from Manchester.

Where it rains.

When on a bright sunny day it's still grey.

And therefore you may spot some rays of northern perspective shining through the pages occasionally.

As I say in my business presentations, if you're looking for some Californian type motivation you're in for a disappointment. This is Mancunian motivation.

Tell it as it is.

No bull.

And let's be really practical. (Oh, and I also try on occasions to inject some humour into what I realize is a potentially heavy subject. To be fair you may or may not spot my attempts.)

So I hope you can cope.

If so, then let's begin.

And remember,

Enjoy the journey.

Paul McGee

For some people, worry, stress and anxiety may be a far more serious issue than can be addressed by simply reading a book. If it is affecting your health or wellbeing, whilst I hope this book does help in some small way I would strongly urge you to seek professional help.

Section One

Stop, Understand

Chapter 1

The Big Deal About Worry

If you're reading this book and you're from what is often described as the developed free world, let me ask you some questions:

How does it feel to be one of the wealthiest people to have ever lived on this planet?

How does it feel to know your life expectancy is higher than any other generation that's ever been born?

How does it feel to have the opportunity to travel and discover more of life's riches in a week than most people previously had in a lifetime?

Now let me ask you another question:

Why on earth, given the above, would anyone need to worry, feel anxious or suffer from stress?

But the fact is we do.

Some argue that our mental wellbeing has never been as fragile as it is now. Newspapers scream headlines of a stress epidemic. Doctors' waiting rooms are full of people suffering less from tangible physical ailments but more from psychological ones.

And despite the current economic gloom, the reality is

we've never had it so good

and yet

we've never felt so bad.

How come?

If you were born in 1900 your life expectancy was around 46. (And if you were born that year then congratulations on living so long – but what possessed you to buy this book?) If you were born in 2003 your life expectancy is now over 80 years.

Good, eh?

Materially we've never had such prosperity. And that's despite the economic turbulence of the last few years.

Technology has transformed our lives. And yes, although it can always be used to bring destruction, in most cases it's used to bring hope, help and convenience to millions of lives.

In a nutshell we're the healthiest and wealthiest generation that's ever lived.

And

we're worrying more.

Survey after survey reports both stress and depression levels are rising.

The medical profession continues to dispense pills and potions at an alarming rate in order to rectify or at least dampen down our anxiety. And now there are even calls for children to be screened for anxiety disorders to prevent them developing mental problems in later life.

In a generation where an overwhelming sense of gratitude should be our defining emotion it seems fear in all its various guises is actually more pervasive.

Strange, isn't it?

But however strange it may be, it's a reality.

This is no half-baked conspiracy theory.

Worry, stress, anxiety or whichever label you prefer to use are real issues.

Not only are they real issues but they have real consequences.

Consequences that ultimately impact not only our lives but also the lives of others around us.

It's a big deal.

With serious implications.

So what do we mean by worry?

My friend Stephanie was curious to know about the book I'm writing. When I mentioned it was on the subject of worry, she replied, 'Oh I don't need to read that – I never worry, it's not in my make up. I get stressed at times and occasionally feel anxious about stuff, but I never worry.'

Well, whatever label you use to describe your emotions, be it worry, stress, nerves or anxiety, they all seem to have common themes. All of them imply a lack of emotional wellbeing to some degree or another.

However, like the words 'love' or 'God' they're often used liberally and without any thought about their real meaning. They're words which mean different things to different people. But as you'd expect, people are not about to sit down and analyze or unpack what they specifically mean. The person experiencing some form of emotional turmoil is unlikely to embark upon the following conversation:

'I'm really worried about my son's exam results. Actually, am I worried? Maybe I'm anxious. Maybe that's a more accurate description

to describe the emotions I'm currently feeling. Or perhaps I'm neither. Maybe I'm stressing about his future and the implications if he doesn't get his grades. Yep, that's it. I'm not worried, I'm not anxious. I'm stressed.'

However, although people use the terms worry, anxiety and stress interchangeably, the following illustrations will clarify in your own mind the differences between them and how they relate to each other.

Worry is a form of thinking. Our mind becomes focused on a particular problem, concern or challenge. How we worry can either be constructive or destructive. There's **'worth it worry'**, which hopefully leads to you taking some form of action to resolve an issue, or there's **'worthless worry'**, which does nothing to actually deal with the concerns you have.

Anxiety is an uncomfortable feeling or emotion. It's that sense of apprehension and dread that something bad is going to happen or something is about to go wrong.

Stress is the body's physical response to a perceived threat. It's often an instantaneous unconscious reaction that is triggered in the primitive part of the brain. This part of the brain's primary goal is to keep you alive, hence the expression 'fight or flight response.' (We'll explore this in a lot more detail later.) Actually, there is a third survival response, which in this context rarely gets a mention, and that is to freeze. Sometimes our ability to keep still and motionless could help protect us from a predator. We share these survival responses with much of the animal kingdom. The primitive part of the brain is also often referred to as the reptilian part of the brain, which gives us a big clue about its evolutionary origins.

So our thinking (worry) leads us to feel (anxiety) which results in a physical response (stress).

However, the root of our problem doesn't always start with worry. It can begin at any part of the cycle.

For instance, my wife and I experienced a rare event in the north west of England one summer – we had over two hours of uninterrupted sunshine. Seizing the moment, we headed for some fields near where we lived in the hope of enjoying a stroll in the sunshine.

It was peaceful and idyllic.

At one stage we even contemplated holding hands.

We saw young children picking blackberries and the sound of an ice cream van announcing its presence in the distance.

Everything was calm and relaxed, and then suddenly, out of nowhere, our lives were in mortal danger.

On the other side of a hedge we were walking past was a huge vicious dog.

It had no lead.

No owner was in sight.

It had only one intention:

to kill my wife

and me.

An unannounced expletive escaped from my mouth.

My hair stood on end.

My heart seemed to awake from its leisurely afternoon.

I could literally feel its desperate attempt to pump blood through my veins, as if my very life depended on it.

My fight or flight response had definitely been activated.

In a nano second

I felt anxious.

I worried that any moment now the dog would attack us.

It didn't.

In fact we never saw it.

Not face to face anyway.

So what did really happen?

Well, most of the above did happen.

I perhaps exaggerated about contemplating holding hands.

But the rest is true.

Almost.

We were walking beside a hedge when we heard the barking of what sounded like a large, vicious and very aggressive dog. I couldn't actually see it as it was on the other side of a tall hedge but I was able to imagine it.

I pictured it without its owner.

Without a lead.

I even imagined what type of dog it was.

And I'm glad I imagined all of the above.

I'm glad my primitive brain was activated and that my body was instantaneously primed to deal with a potential physical attack.

Because if it was true I was in the most appropriate physical state to deal with the challenge.

This might seem strange in the light of some literature on the subject, but stress was my friend.

Feeling anxious felt entirely appropriate and worrying about our possible escape route and whether there was an opening in the hedge kept me focused and alert.

In this instance it was stress that triggered the cycle.

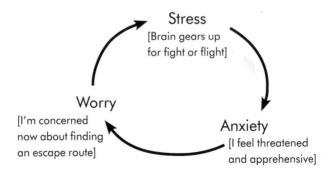

On other occasions we feel anxious for no apparent reason. We just sense intuitively that things are not right or something is wrong. We begin to worry as our mind wrestles with an unidentified problem.

This in turn triggers a stress response as our body experiences an increased heart rate, our pupils dilate and our chest tightens.

There are times when at a conscious level we're not sure why we're feeling the way we are and the term we use to describe how we're feeling may vary from person to person.

'I'm nervous.'

'I'm feeling really tense at the moment.'

'I'm stressed out.'

'I'm really anxious.'

'I'm worried about all sorts.'

Understandably in such a situation we don't take time to analyze our feelings and the accuracy of the terms used to describe them; we simply express them.

In this instance the cycle looks like this:

Sometimes there can be a clear reason for your anxiety. For example, imagine you're about to attend an important work meeting. You're feeling anxious because you know there will be a number of very senior people there. You're keen to impress. You're even keener not to make a mistake, say anything inappropriate or appear foolish in any way. But you begin to worry about the meeting. Questions buzz around you like an annoying wasp. 'What if I clam up? What if I'm asked a question and I don't know the answer? What if no one speaks to me?' As a result your anxiety increases. You sweat more, your mouth is dry, you feel awful.

So, given that people use different words to describe similar feelings or emotional states, for the purpose of this book I will refer to each term interchangeably. Ultimately the issue is not that we use the correct terminology, but more importantly that we understand the causes and the impact of worry, anxiety and stress, and why it's become such a big deal. Agree?

So what's the impact of worrying?

When we worry it's like the engine of our mind is constantly being revved up. Worry and anxiety don't allow us time to switch off and rest. They don't allow us time to enjoy the journey.

Another analogy is that of an elastic band. It was designed to be stretched, but stretch it too far or for too long and it weakens. Likewise we can thrive on pressure. It's good for our own wellbeing if we're stretched at times. But stretch us too much for too long and healthy pressure can become unhealthy stress. We can weaken psychologically and emotionally. And if we're not careful, like that elastic band we can end up snapping.

Worry can weaken us.

It can lead to a decrease in our sex drive.

Too much strain and stress weakens our immune system. We're more prone to sickness. We're using our thoughts and imagination about our future, not to inspire and motivate us, but to rob us of a sense of calm by focusing on potential problems, challenges and threats.

And we're using our thoughts and imagination about past events to do the same.

You could describe worry, anxiety and stress as an unholy trinity. They're not quite the axis of evil threatening world peace, but they can, when left unchecked, threaten and undermine our own sense of personal peace.

> When you're worrying about the future you're missing out on the joys of the present

Worry drains us of energy. *Energy for life.*

Can you relate to mental as well as physical fatigue?

Yes?

Well, that's what worry can do to you.

It tires you out.

And when you're tired you're less likely to think straight.

And when you're not thinking straight it's easy to make stupid mistakes. To react to the world as you see it rather than respond to how it actually is.

The bottom line?

Stress makes you stupid.

And it can make you sick.

Stupid and sick. Some cocktail, eh?

Give me a piña colada any day.

But without realizing it we order up ourselves a large worry cocktail.

It's the costliest one on the menu

and we don't even know we're paying for it.

But we are.

Big time.

We're paying for it with our sense of peace.

We're paying for it with the quality of our relationships.

We're paying for it with our health.

Worry robs us of the energy to focus on the 'today' in order to create a better 'tomorrow.'

How can you enjoy the moment when you're worried about the future or trapped in the past?

Given enough time worry becomes a habit. A label. If we're not careful worry can become our identity. We might as well introduce ourselves as 'Hello, I'm a worrier. Pleased to meet you.' Some people live life as if they've got a PhD in worrying. In fact they start becoming anxious and restless when they don't have anything to worry about. Like smoking, some people have become addicted to it. They need it. And despite the negative consequences they seem unable or perhaps unwilling to kick the worry habit. Something we'll explore in more detail later.

So does worry ever work?

Absolutely. If a certain degree of worry motivates you to tackle problems in a productive manner then clearly it's been a positive catalyst towards change. When that's the case, great. It's what I referred to earlier as **'worth it worry'**. But the reality is that worry and anxiety are far more likely to disable you than enable you. Rather than help put you in a prime state to tackle your challenges, they instead unnerve and unbalance you.

That's the problem.

We've become used to a way of handling challenges that brings more harm than good.

But relax.

There is a way forward.

There is a way to use a certain degree of worry and anxiety to spur us on towards positive, constructive action. There is a way to tackle life's challenges in a calmer and more considered way. However, if you're looking for the recipe for a worry- and stress-free existence, you're reading the wrong book. If that's the case I'd quit reading now if I were you. You'll be disappointed and disillusioned if that's what you're after. I'm in pursuit of a more practical approach.

We need challenge.

We need pressure.

We need to be stretched.

It's what makes us human. It's part of our evolutionary make up.

Remember that elastic band analogy? It was designed to be stretched. A limp elastic band is not much good to anyone. Right?

So the antidote to our anxieties is not a life of relaxation, reclining on a beach, sipping our favourite drink, listening to our favourite music whilst the waves of the sea lap up along the shore.

Honestly it isn't.

You may think it is.

And for some people that is their antidote.

For a while.

But trust me, that lifestyle can get monotonous.

Great for a few days.

Maybe even a couple of weeks.

But life often becomes boring when you've nothing to do. When you've nothing to focus your mind on. When there's no particular reason for getting out of bed in the morning.

You see we need a purpose if we're to function effectively as people.

It's not a blissful state of nirvana we're after. It's a sense of meaning.

A reason to be here.

On this planet.

Right now.

That's what we're really aiming for.

Not less pressure.

More purpose.

And with that purpose will come a need to deal with challenges, to seize opportunities, to take risks, to do things that at times make us feel uncomfortable.

That's what energizes our existence.

That's what we're really after.

Not stress free.

And along the way we'll need time out for rest and recovery. And we'll need to call upon all the resources imbued upon us from birth to fulfil our purpose in life.

And we'll also need to take care as well as take risks.

Because if we don't we'll find our biological make up that has evolved and developed over thousands of years to help equip us for survival can actually hinder our path to success.

How come? Well stay tuned because we're going to explore more about this a little later in the book.

The reality is the key to conquering our worries and to reducing our levels of stress and anxiety is not a strategy of elimination or avoidance.

It's about understanding.

It's about awareness.

It's about gaining an insight into how we function best as people. It's about acquiring the knowledge necessary to enable us to fulfil our potential as people. To enjoy, not simply endure the ride.

And when the game of life as we know it is over I want to share similar sentiments to the unknown author of this piece:

> *'Life should not be a journey to the grave with the intention of arriving safely in an attractive and well presented body; but rather to skid in sideways, chocolate in one hand, wine in the other, body thoroughly used up, totally worn out and screaming "Woo hoo, what a ride!"'*

I love that piece. I want to capture some of that spirit and essence in my life. It might not be wine and chocolate that floats your boat – but your goal is to find out what does.

We've all been given this amazing opportunity.

It's called life.

It comes with amazing possibilities.

It will inevitably include some heartache and setbacks along the way.

But it doesn't come with a clear set of instructions.

They're for us to discover.

And sadly the lessons we learn from others are not always helpful.

Sometimes we fail to learn from our own mistakes.

And what equipped us to deal with life just ten years ago may no longer be enough now.

The world is changing.

Rapidly.

Some of us are struggling to keep up.

Some of us are on the sidelines being held back from participating.

And what's holding us back?

Worry.

Anxiety.

Stress.

Do you know what the big deal is?

The big deal about worry is that it robs us of living a meaningful and worthwhile life.

It robs us of enjoyment.

It robs us of a sense of peace and wellbeing.

That's a big deal in my book.

And so that's why we're going to spend time understanding the reasons behind our worries, and learn techniques and ideas on how to deal with it effectively.

Life can be a bit of a rollercoaster at times.

Are you ready to engage in and enjoy the ride?

Great. Then let's begin with understanding the reasons why worry, anxiety and stress can put the brakes on our momentum and ultimately derail us.

Chapter 2

Why Do We Worry?

Right. Time to analyze why in fact we do worry. The act of worrying is not something bestowed upon us at birth like a birth mark or the colour of our eyes. It's not some medical defect that either you have or you haven't got.

There are reasons.

In fact, there could be lots of reasons.

Most of which you've never really sat down and thought about.

Well, now's your chance.

Let's explore nine reasons that could contribute to you feeling worried, anxious or stressed. We'll cover eight in this chapter and devote a whole chapter to the ninth.

Firstly though, a couple of what at first may seem rather bizarre and pointless questions. Let me reassure you they're not.

When you walk down stairs which foot do you tend to lead with, the right or the left?

When you're chewing your food which side of your mouth do you use most, the right or the left?

That's it. You can relax now. No more questioning at this stage.

OK, so will your answers to the above provide you with a fascinating and remarkable insight about your character and personality?

Actually, no.

But they will reveal something, however.

My guess is you didn't automatically and instinctively know the answers to the above questions.

You had to think about it.

This is in spite of the fact that eating food and walking downstairs is something you do every day. (OK, you may live in a bungalow and exist on a diet of soup and milkshakes, but you get my point.)

The reality is you do both activities without thinking about what you're doing.

It's not a conscious decision.

You do it on autopilot.

Without thinking.

We do that a lot.

We spend a lot of time living on autopilot.

Doing things.

Going to places.

Eating stuff.

Without consciously thinking what we're doing

or

why we're doing it.

Worrying is a bit like that.

You don't consciously decide to worry.

It's not a case of 'It's Monday, that's worry day. Can't stop. Got lots of worrying to do.'

Worry can become a habit. A spontaneous reaction to a situation. The real truth is:

> We can actually feel worried and anxious about something and not be aware of the reasons why

But by bringing to the surface the reasons why we do worry you've more chance of dealing with it.

After all, you can choose to chew your food with the opposite side of your mouth and set off downstairs with your other foot.

The consequences of doing so are unlikely to make a deep and profound impact on your life, but the point is you do have choices. You can make changes.

But understanding why we worry and then doing something about it – well, that's a different ball game entirely.

That can have a profound impact on your life. Agree?

Right, let's get started with that list.

Here goes.

Remember, these are *possible* reasons why people worry.

The first reason will I'm sure surprise you.

1. We can enjoy worrying

'Surely not?' I hear you cry. Actually it's true. Now it might be happening at a subconscious level, but for some people worrying gives their lives a sense of purpose and drama. Let's be honest, living on planet Earth is not always a back-to-back experience of high drama and entertainment, is it?

I'm sure we all have our moments.

Some more than others.

But can I be brutally frank and open here?

There's much of my life where words such as 'routine' and 'mundane' are about as exciting as it gets.

And if that summarizes where a lot of people are at the majority of the time, then the conversation can get a little dull at times, can't it?

That's why people such as myself can ramble on for hours about football.

That's why television soaps are popular.

They engage us.

They entertain.

They give us something to talk about.

But sometimes that's not enough.

We want to be the star of the show.

We want to be in the spotlight.

We want to be a part of the drama.

And what's a surefire indicator that the above is happening?

When we worry, of course.

We rarely worry about the routine and the mundane.

So *on certain occasions* when we are worrying, perhaps that's another way of saying that our lives have taken a detour off that road marked 'nothing particularly exciting or memorable is happening in my life.'

Maybe we need that release of cortisol and rush of adrenalin.

It keeps us on our toes.

Some people seek thrills on a fairground ride.

Others pursue extreme sports.

And others have the uncanny ability to turn trivia into tragedy.

To create a crisis from a place of calm.

Perhaps worrying provides some people with a sense of significance and purpose.

Possibly?

Maybe they're not consciously aware they're doing it, but at a subconscious level worrying is actually meeting some kind of need.

Believable?

I think so.

That's why some people, despite their protestations, have no intention of kicking the worry habit.

They may even read this book.

You may even lend them your copy..

 But do you know what?

It won't work.

'I tried reading the book. But it hasn't worked. They never do. I must be a special case.'

Really? You think you're a special case, do you?

Maybe for some people worry works.

They like it that way.

Don't provide me with a solution.

Don't give me ideas and insights to tackle my problem. Then what will I do? Go back to mundane and routine?

No thank you.

Give me drama any day. Even if it doesn't exist. I'll create some.

I have to.

I need that rush.

You see, there are biological reasons why people enjoy some stress in their lives. The hormones adrenaline and noradrenaline released by our adrenal glands when we feel stressed can stimulate us and make us feel energized and even powerful. For a while. Some people can actually become addicted to this stress rush. But if bungee jumping and sky diving are not an option then I'll seek out stress elsewhere. I'll create it if I have to. It's my way of feeding my habit. Of feeling important.

Remember, I'm not suggesting this is the main reason why all people worry, but do you know anyone who might be worrying because secretly, deep down, they actually enjoy it?

2. The challenge of change and uncertainty

I heard the following statement recently that made me smile:

> I wouldn't mind change if everything wasn't so different afterwards

If only it was that easy.

Charles Darwin, however, made a hugely important point regarding change. *'It is not the strongest of the species that survive, nor the most intelligent, but the one most responsive to change.'*

Interesting, eh?

Ultimately our very survival is dependent on our ability to adapt to change. But I think most people could quite happily cope with a large dose of certainty and stability, at least for a while, rather than the current sustained assault of uncertainty and constant change.

Questions such as:

How secure is my job?

Will there be another recession?

Can I pay the credit card bills this month?

What about my kids' future?

Can I cope with all this change?

can race around our minds incessantly. These are genuine concerns. This is not irrational thinking on our part. This is not a need to create drama.

This is a reality.

This is the 21st century. And the rate of change can be overwhelming. And although we at times crave excitement and are enticed by the new and novel, there can be something hugely comforting in the old and the familiar. In the stable. In the status quo. But at the moment there seems to be less of that on the menu. Change and uncertainty seem to be the main dishes for both main course and dessert. And some people are failing to thrive on such a diet.

Here's the third reason.

3. A lack of knowledge and experience

Sometimes our reasons for worrying are rather straightforward. We've been asked to do something that we've never done before. We're faced with a challenge we haven't previously encountered.

We're involved in a situation we're not sure how to handle. In other words we lack the knowledge or know-how.

It's not a question of which tools shall I use – we're not sure if we've even got the right tool box.

When that's the case feelings of tension and uncertainty are both natural and normal.

We like to be in control.

To know what we're doing.

To feel we can handle a situation.

So when we're in new territory,

when we're out of our comfort zone,

we can feel a little anxious.

We may act confident.

We may even display some bravado.

But deep down we know our esteem could be about to take a knock.

You see, when you throw someone in the deep end without any life aids they rarely learn to swim.

They drown.

And if we're having to make things up as we go along because no one is offering us support or showing us how best to approach things, then we're probably going to feel a little threatened.

We don't like to look stupid.

It damages our ego.

That's understandable.

In fact, it's perfectly understandable.

So if you're faced with a situation where you've no previous experience and little or no idea how to deal with it, then a rush of anxiety is a natural response.

In fact, if you don't feel at least a little uncomfortable about the situation then you've clearly failed to grasp the facts! The real truth is this:

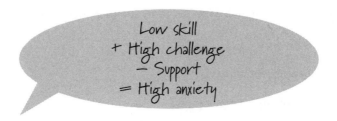

Low skill
+ High challenge
− Support
= High anxiety

But although you may crave the need to feel confident in order to eliminate your worry, it's actually competence you need. Once you've gained competence, i.e. the knowledge, experience and ability, then confidence will follow and your anxiety should decrease.

Indeed, anxiety and worry arising from a lack of knowledge and experience is something I can very much relate to. One particularly stressful time in my life springs to mind.

I was weeks away from my 18th birthday.

A levels were over, the sunshine was out and long lazy summer days lay ahead.

For most of my mates.

But I was starting a new job.

Desiring nothing more than to be an actor or a journalist I started off my working career as a bank clerk.

It seemed like a good idea at the time.

At least to my family and teachers at school.

I was less convinced.

But caught up in a wave of 'You're lucky to have a job and you're not clever enough to go to university', I found myself leaving home at 7.30am on a Monday morning to begin life in a bank.

I was nervous.

Most people would be.

I was out of my comfort zone.

I was facing the unknown.

Within 30 minutes I felt overwhelmed by what was expected of me and underwhelmed by the potential job satisfaction I would achieve.

It seemed I was neither mentally nor physically equipped to carry out the duties required of a bank clerk in the 1980s.

I felt like a one-armed man trying to thread a needle.

I was simply not cut out for the job.

My colleagues tried to reassure me.

'A monkey blindfolded could do this job' was the reassuring comment of Jackie on my first day.

Really?

Looks like I'm dumber than a blind monkey then.

Maybe the bank should change their recruitment policy and target zoos rather than schools in the future.

You see, if you've being doing the same job for a few years then I guess there does come a time when you can do it blindfolded almost, whether you're a monkey or not.

But I was new.

Everything was new to me. The people. The job. The pace of work. The daily routine.

I had been articulate at interview, but they hadn't tested for manual dexterity.

They hadn't assessed my quest for accuracy and my ability to work under pressure.

My comfort zone seemed like a distant shoreline somewhere over the horizon whilst I was stranded on some remote and deserted island.

My toilet habits changed.

Sorry to be so crude but they did.

Toilet paper sales soared in a certain suburb of South Manchester.

I hated it. (Not South Manchester, the job.)

I hated the overwhelming sense of anxiety I felt.

I hated the sense of turning up for work to do a job I didn't enjoy and wasn't good at doing.

The 1982 World Cup offered some respite.

But not enough.

My unhappiness even affected my relationships at home.

And I came to realize this.

No amount of meditation, positive thinking and relaxing in a hot bath would ease my anxiety.

The root of any worries, anxieties and stress could not be resolved with such an approach.

My problem was deeper.

I either needed to acquire a range of abilities and skills that up to that point I didn't possess, or I needed to leave.

I chose the latter.

Within days I found myself back to my old self.

Sales of toilet paper plummeted.

And I had learnt a huge lesson.

Sometimes you have to admit that treating the symptoms of our worry isn't enough. We have to get to the root of the problem. And sometimes admitting defeat could actually open the door to finding success elsewhere.

Hammock time

Right, here's your opportunity to take some time out to reflect on what you've read so far. So far we've explored three reasons as to why people may worry. Here's a recap.

1 We can enjoy worrying.
2 The challenge of change and uncertainty.
3 A lack of knowledge and experience.

- So which of the above can you relate to in particular?
- Is there a sense in which you relate to the fact that you actually quite enjoy the adrenalin rush when you're worrying or feeling stressed? Do you know anyone who does?
- Are you facing a lot of change and uncertainty at present? If so, how well do you feel able to cope?
- Has there been a time when you've felt a lack of experience and knowledge has resulted in you becoming anxious and stressed? How have you handled this previously?
- What support did you receive when this happened?

Right, now onto the next three.

4. A lack of influence or control

To some extent we're all control freaks. Certainly compared to the rest of the animal kingdom we are. We like to feel we have at least some degree of control in a situation. It's fair to say that some people display this side of their personality in a much more extreme way than others and the term 'freak' is perhaps a little strong. But the truth is the majority of us like to be in control. Which may explain why the majority of us like to choose our own lottery numbers rather than being given them randomly by a machine. Neither way makes any real difference, but by choosing our own numbers we feel a greater sense of control, of our destiny.

And if you need any more convincing then check out the behaviour of a toddler and how they seek to exert their control over their parents, especially when they don't want to eat or be put in a car seat!

Now whether or not you're a fan of Formula 1 motor racing, it's fair to say that being a driver can be a stressful experience. However, I understand drivers experience one of their highest levels of stress during the race not on the first bend but at the pit stop.

Why?

They weren't in control.

They were relying on someone else.

Can you relate to that?

Have you ever got stressed at an airport because your flight is delayed?

Ever found yourself stressing due to the late arrival of a taxi?

And why is moving house considered such a stressful experience?

Because there's so much that has to happen that is outside your control.

Your sale may fall through and there could be absolutely nothing you could do about it.

That lack of influence of control particularly in relation to what could be considered a significant life experience is not comfortable. You may have invested not just large amounts of money into this forthcoming move but equally large amounts of emotional energy.

And yet the final outcome could ultimately be entirely out of your hands.

So what happens when we lack control over something significant and important to us?

Cue the anxiety.

Cue the stress rising.

Cue the interrupted sleep due to worry.

The truth is:

> The less control you have in a situation, the more likely you are to worry

And as we'll see later the issue is all about your perceived sense of control.

Perception is reality. The problem is you might have a faulty perception of a situation.

You may have more control or influence than you realize.

It doesn't matter.

It's your perception that counts.

It's not the facts.

It's your perception of the facts that is the key.

So how do we seize some form of control? We worry. We feel that by worrying about a situation we are in some way influencing it.

There's a story told of a man in India who would throw bits of paper out of the window when travelling by train. "Why are you doing that?" a fellow passenger asked. "I'm keeping elephants off the tracks" was his reply. "But there are no elephants on the railway line." "I know. It must be working."

And the point of the story?

Perhaps in a less obvious way people delude themselves into believing that by simply worrying about a situation they are in some way influencing the outcome. And then live with the illusion that because they worried about something and it didn't happen then worry obviously works. (Like paper keeping away the elephants.)

Here's the fifth reason for why people worry.

5. Your values

Have you ever met anyone who rarely seems to worry?

Have you met someone who seems to drift along in life whilst those around them flap around in a constant state of near panic?

And the reason?

Well, there could be several. But this one may surprise you.

The person who rarely worries *could* be the person who rarely cares. Their lack of worry could be embedded within their attitudes to life.

What other people think of them is not important.

Being late is a fact of life.

Live for today, forget tomorrow.

The difference as to why some people worry and others don't is often down to values and what's important to people.

Some of my friends worry about the state of their car. I see it as less of a priority. A scratch can signal anger or even panic for them. I see it as a fact of life.

You see, it's not about being right or wrong. It's simply that when we care a lot about something or someone we are potentially more prone to worrying.

Having worked as a probation officer in the 1980s I was amazed at the relaxed attitude some people had about the whereabouts of their young children. I'm not sure if such a mindset was born out of ignorance, culture or values – perhaps it was all three – but I personally would not swap their carefree attitude for my anxiety if I was unaware of where my small child was.

Maybe worrying to some extent is the price we pay for our values. The question is, is it too high a price to pay on occasions? And is what we consider to be important really that important?

Is a small scratch on the car or the unexpected arrival of friends when the house looks a tip a reason for a stress party?

Is it really?

Or are we allowing our values to hold our anxiety levels hostage?

Remember next time you find yourself worrying, maybe it would be useful to acknowledge the root of this is born out of the fact that you care.

Fine.

But can caring go too far? I think so.

Clearly worrying about a loved one can be seen as a sign we care. For instance, a parent's love for their children is understandable, but if you're continually telling your 49-year-old son or daughter to wrap up warm because it's cold outside you've possibly crossed the boundary of just caring. Indicating your concern over something quite trivial and excusing yourself by saying you're worried about their welfare is in fact conveying a message that implies they're not capable of dressing themselves properly. That's fine when they're five, but not 49. Maybe it's time to give worry a break and allow your caring to be expressed in a different way.

Agree?

OK, now onto a slightly more controversial one.

6. Your upbringing

Research indicates that a stressful pregnancy may in fact lead to a stressful baby. It's not inevitable but it's certainly possible. However, perhaps more significant is how the baby and young child are brought up.

A stressed parent or carer will invariably transmit their stress onto their children.

Children take their cues from their parents.

If Mum, Dad or any other care giver sees the world as a hostile place, a young child is unlikely to respond 'Hey, relax guys. You watch too much news. Grab a beer, take a chill pill and let's play pool.' Well, my two certainly didn't.

If my parents and carers exhibit anxiety and I'm aware of it, then guess what?

There's an increased likelihood I'll be anxious also.

I'll suck up some of your stress.

And although you may not realize it, Mum, Dad, Grandma, Granddad, or any other nurturers in my life – you're my main role models. I learn through mimicking. I copy you.

I don't weigh up and assess your strategies for dealing with life and say "You know what: I think that's a complete overreaction to the situation. It's just a spider for goodness sake. And as for your money problems, forget denial as a way forward, you need to tackle this stuff before it gets way out of hand."

I simply copy what you do.

Your strategies for life become mine.

I don't question them.

I just absorb them.

Certainly to begin with.

And I might find them hard to shake off.

Even if they're lousy strategies.

So if you make mountains out of molehills, the odds are that so will I.

If you see the world as a nasty place with a potential evil predator around each corner, guess what?

So will I.

And if you let me watch the news and crime shows and don't explain stuff to me then you're laying down some pretty deep and solid foundations on which I can build my worry house.

Is all the above inevitable?

No.

But here's the real truth:

> We are role models to our kids, whether we intend to be or not

We will never be perfect.

And what I don't want to do is cause you even more stress and anxiety because you're now feeling guilty about your parenting skills!

But I do want to challenge you.

Dealing with your own stress levels isn't just good for you.

It's good for everyone.

Especially your kids.

If you have them, that is.

And even if you don't have children, be aware of how your upbringing has affected you.

That's not an excuse.

Neither is it an opportunity to blame someone else.

But it is one reason (and there will be more) why you might worry about stuff more than other people.

Hammock time

Let's review our last three reasons for why we may worry:

1 A lack of influence or control.
2 Our values.
3 Our upbringing.

Now think about the following questions:

- On a scale of 1-10 (where 10 is high) how much would you rate yourself as a controller?
- Does this vary depending on whether you're at home or work?
- In what ways can you relate to not being in control affecting your stress levels?
- Reflect on how your values affect your anxiety levels. Is there any area of your life on which you place too much significance and importance ? Perhaps that is a difficult one to answer for ourselves, so who could give you their perspective which you might find helpful?

> • How would you describe your upbringing in terms of how others around you responded to challenges?
> • Can you identify any unhelpful habits that you realize you've picked up from your parents? (Although it's easier to pick them up than to put them down, it is possible to change your ways. Look for ideas in this book to help you.)

OK, now onto the next two reasons why people worry.

7. Previous experiences

My daughter was once bitten by a dog. It was actually just a nip but she was only around three years old at the time. She was nervous of dogs for a long time after that. No amount of reassurance would help. Friendly-looking dogs, no matter what their size, could still be the potential source of pain.

Previous experience had taught her that.

When I was ten years old I played the role of Buttons in the school pantomime production of *Cinderella*. There were four acts in total. I didn't take part at all in the third act. So I relaxed and played cards with a friend in one of the classrooms whilst the other actors were on stage.

But I lost track of time.

Act four started. I was still playing cards. It got to my line.

Problem was I wasn't on stage to deliver it. I was still playing cards.

Mayhem ensued.

The audience waited

for the next line,

and then someone shouted

"Buttons!"

I put down my cards. It was a good hand.

A teacher glared at me. I can still see their face today.

I ran on stage and delivered my line.

Act four finished.

I felt humiliated.

My parents came that night.

I won't forget it.

I'd like to.

But I won't.

It happened over 35 years ago. Yet even today I can find myself worrying about being late. Not for stuff that I don't consider important. But for the stuff that is I find my anxiety levels can soar if I'm delayed and don't actively seek to control them. The memory of playing Buttons still haunts me.

Here's the real truth:

Your past can still have a profound impact on your present

It might not be rational

but it's real.

If you've had an experience that ended painfully it's probably put paid to you feeling positive about a similar one in the future.

And interestingly the previous experience doesn't even have to be your own.

My friend Andy has wrestled for years about having a vasectomy. Andy's problem is that he still has a rather painful memory of his mate Kev having a similar operation several years ago. Without going into too much detail, the outcome of Kev's operation was not the most comfortable experience of his life, even two weeks after the event. Many men having a similar operation will feel fine and dandy within a few days. But when things go well people don't think to talk about it. So Andy's only reference point was Kev.

Kev chose not to take the stiff upper lip approach to his pain and therefore spared Andy none of the gory details. The thought of having a similar operation filled Andy with dread and when he finally decided to go ahead with it he described his anxiety levels as being higher than the Eiffel tower!

The above examples, while real, are also to a degree amusing (although Andy might not agree). However, for some people their previous experiences could actually be categorized as traumatic. Those who have suffered trauma, especially early in life, tend to be more anxious than those who haven't. Such experiences make the brain even more vigilant and wary of potential problems.

My friend Anne was involved in a car accident, and although she overcame her fear of being in a car again, the traumatic episode of her past influenced her levels of anxiety in the present. Although such anxiety can be managed and avoidance of going in a car will only exacerbate Anne's situation, it is highly insensitive to trivialize the worries and concerns that some people have which may have arisen out of previous painful experience.

Right, now onto our final reason. It's unlikely to make me popular amongst some journalists, but here goes...

8. Overexposure to bad news

I enjoy reading. I particularly enjoy reading the Sunday paper. I always start with the sports section – an experience which is always enhanced if Bradford City or my son's team Wigan Athletic have avoided defeat the previous day. However, I rarely watch the news these days as it seems the internet can provide me with the headline stuff that I need to know.

So when a story breaks about some horrific child abduction or some senseless act of violence I choose to be aware of the story but not immersed in it.

I appreciate that my approach is not shared by everyone. Some people consume news like I consume chocolate. (Only vanity about my waistline prevents this from becoming a 24-hour habit.)

But could the media, in whichever form we access it, be contributing to our worries? Are we being bombarded with a huge amount of frightening but mostly irrelevant information?

It's a challenging and maybe controversial question, but is the media messing us up by feeding our fears?

And if so, why?

Here's the deal.

Fear sells.

Imagine you're a charity desperately seeking increased funding and profile.

What do you do?

Saturate the media with good news stories about the work you've done?

Great. Sounds good.

It may even get you some coverage.

For a day.

But then what? How do you maximize your coverage?

How do you get the media and general public to sit up and take notice?

Here's how.

Tell scary stories.

The real truth is:

Fear is a great marketing tool.
A scare story gets our attention.
Good news rarely does

We're wired to take note of anything that might be a potential threat.

The media knows that.

It's in competition for our eyes and our ears. So it does what you would expect it to do.

It responds to our rising fears and worries.

A person is tragically killed by a shark whilst on honeymoon.

That's terrible.

It's front-page news.

The next day the media extends its coverage of shark attacks around the world. And for the next few days any attack, no matter how minor, will be reported.

Our media responds to our rising fear by reporting on it more. And so begins the worry cycle.

More worry, more reporting, more reporting, more worry. Couple that with our oversensitive primitive brain (we'll look at this more in our next chapter) and you've got yourself a large worry cocktail.

Worry and anxiety can spread like a virus, and the media is one of the primary channels for helping it to do so.

As a result we overestimate the likelihood of being killed by the things that make the news ('Don't swim in the sea, there could be sharks') and underestimate those that don't.

What makes the news?

The rare, the vivid, the catastrophic.

If it bleeds it leads.

Diabetes, asthma and heart disease are less in vogue.

Bovine spongiform encephalopathy is.

But people won't remember that even if we call it BSE. So what does David Brown, writing for the *Daily Telegraph*, decide to call it?

Mad cow disease.

We like that.

It's memorable.

It engages us.

Diabetes and heart disease don't.

But which is the biggest killer? Which threatens us most?

I guess the media, in a desire to grab our attention, taps into something known as the Von Restorff effect – a bias in favour of remembering the unusual.

And so we worry about stuff that will rarely happen, if ever. But because the news and entertainment shows feed us bad news, we tend to think it's more likely to occur. It's what psychologists call *'the illusion of truth effect.'* If we hear something repeatedly it becomes familiar. We like familiar, and because familiar information requires less effort to process we assume it to be true. So eventually we stop questioning what we're hearing or reading.

And even good news gets distorted.

Death due to cancer is on the rise. Why?

Because we're living longer.

That should be good news.

It is.

But cancer is more prevalent amongst the elderly population. Hence it's on the rise.

It's also on the increase because other killers such as TB or smallpox have virtually been eliminated.

Again, good news.

But that doesn't make us sit up and take notice.

So what does the media do?

Accentuate the negative and play down the positive.

By doing so it taps into our innate desire to be told and to tell dramatic stories.

Who needs data that puts everything into perspective and should allay our fears when we can provide a moving and tragic anecdote?

The bottom line is that good new is hard to sell.

Bad news isn't.

We manipulate the media and the media manipulates us.

But the inevitable consequence of this is we get a distorted picture of life and its potential threats, and the noise of media-fuelled scare stories drowns out the cries of what should really concern us.

As a result we worry more. But about the wrong things.

Hammock time

Time to reflect on the last two reasons as to why people worry, become anxious and suffer from stress.

The two were:

1. Previous experience.
2. Overexposure to bad news.

- So have you had a previous painful experience that still causes you a degree of anxiety now? (Don't worry if you don't – I was just asking.)
- (Perhaps you're anxious about something that you've only just realized was triggered by a previous experience that happened to you or someone close to you. But knowing the reason might now help you tackle the issue rather than just thinking it's part of your personality that you cannot change.)
- What positive lessons can you take from a previous experience that can equip you to deal with worry more effectively now?
- How much news do you consume?
- Would you describe yourself as someone who is aware of bad news stories or do you tend to immerse yourself in them?
- How helpful would it be for you in managing and reducing your worry to actually reduce your intake of bad news?

Do women worry more than men?

Finally, to complete this chapter on why people worry, let's look at the contentious issue of whether one sex worries more than the other.

Well, the debate continues to rage as to whether or not women do worry more than men. From evolutionary factors, brain wiring and hormonal levels, various experts put forth their hypothesis.

But the jury is still out.

What does seem clear, however, is that men and women worry in different ways. For instance, the Rush University medical centre in Chicago found through imaging techniques that when women worry they use both the left and right side of the brain.

Men mostly use their left side. The more analytical part of the brain.

Women therefore seem more engaged in their worries from a whole brain perspective than men and by doing so seem to experience worry and negative emotions more intensely.

Clearly this is not always the case but the overall picture does seem to indicate this. It's further argued that women are more likely to verbalize and discuss their worries than men, therefore concluding that women do in fact worry more.

Wrong.

Women may talk openly (and perhaps more honestly) about their worries than men but that does not mean men worry less.

Men can still experience obsessive thoughts and concerns about themselves (their appearance, their health, their families and their future, particularly in relation to finances), but they're less likely to be open about it.

To put it perhaps a little crudely, women talk, men walk. And the walk may entail a trip to the pub, the movies, or to watch a game, where upon arrival they will want to leave their worries behind rather than talk about them.

But they still worry.

But they may often keep quiet about their worries because societal expectations places pressure on men to be seen as copers. To be strong.

Worrying can be seen as a sign of weakness.

When that trait is seen in a woman it can elicit a supportive, caring response.

But when it's seen in a man it can elicit a degree of ridicule and pity in some instances.

So don't expect men to spout off their worries to other men with perhaps the same sense of ease and gusto as their female counterparts do.

Men are also more likely to express their worry and anxiety by projecting it onto others by becoming angry and irritable. So they may be perceived as having an anger problem rather than a worry problem.

And finally, our evolutionary ancestors may also play a part in why women are perceived to worry more than men.

Research conducted by Kristin Lagattula, Associate Professor of Psychology at the University of California Davis (featured in *Child Development Journal* **78** (5), 2007), found that females from childhood to adulthood make stronger connections between bad events in the past and possible negative events in the future. From an evolutionary perspective this may have been important in terms of raising and protecting offspring, which thousands of years later is still seen in many cultures as the main responsibility of the female. This may explain why women generally seem to worry more about their children than their fathers do.

So on the surface women do seem to worry more than men, but dig a little deeper and things are not so cut and dried.

Ultimately, though, whatever our gender, worry or whatever term we choose to call it can, when left unchecked, have a hugely negative impact on us.

Whether you're male or female

worry is a big deal.

So we've explored eight reasons why we worry. Let's remind ourselves of them:

1. We can enjoy worrying

2. The challenge of change and uncertainty

3. A lack of knowledge and experience

4. A lack of influence and control

5. Your values

6. Your upbringing

7. Previous experiences

8. Overexposure to bad news

If you had to identify the three main reasons why you worry, what would they be?

1.

2.

3.

But there's one major reason why we worry that we've yet to explore. I think it's worthy of its own separate chapter. Ready to explore the ninth reason? Good, because if you're like me you'll find this next reason particularly fascinating.

Chapter 3

Are We Wired to Worry?

OK, let me take you back a few years. In fact, let me take you back more than a few years.

Let's go back 50,000 years.

We're back to our prehistoric days.

We're in the hunter gatherer stage of our human evolutionary cycle.

Imagine a bloke who is part of a tribe of nomadic *Homo sapiens*.

Let's call him Bob.

Bob is a laid back optimist.

He sees very little point in worrying about stuff.

His attitude to life is 'Whatever will be, will be.'

And if he's out with his tribe somewhere on the African Savannah and is confronted by a sabre-toothed tiger, a woolly mammoth or whatever else was stalking the place at the time, Bob maintains his optimistic but perhaps also rather complacent outlook on life.

'Look, I was born lucky. If anyone of us is going to die it's bound to be Frank. I mean, look at him. The guy's a loser. He's constantly fretting. He's a nervous wreck. Every day he wakes up he's talking about the need for safety and precaution. His glass isn't half full. No way. He hasn't even got a glass. What Barbara sees in him I'll never know.'

It's now 24 hours later.

You're at a funeral.

It's Bob's.

Frank is saying the final blessing before Bob's body (or what remains of it after his run-in with the tiger) is laid to rest.

Bye, Bob.

Frank looks around at the rest of the tribe.

'Anyone want Bob's "Don't worry, be happy" badge?'

You see, here's the simple fact of life.

Bob is not your ancestor. But Frank might be. Bob definitely isn't.

Bob's genes died out years ago.

They had to.

Bob, not Frank, was the actual loser.

There was something wrong with his wiring.

His laid-back, optimistic and complacent attitude to life was a recipe for death. He'd become mincemeat for mammoths.

Frank's was a recipe for survival.

One of the greatest and most important emotions passed onto Frank by his ancestors was fear.

It can be a constructive emotion. (Frank's badge would read 'I'd rather be fearful and alive than complacent and dead.')

Now our relationship with fear has gone a little haywire in recent years, but it's initial purpose was to alert us to danger and equip us to deal with a potential attack or threat.

That was a very good thing. Ask Frank.

And worry today can have its place. When we worry or become anxious about a potential risk we pay more attention to it. It can motivate us to take action. That's good. That's **'worth it worry'**.

The real truth is …

> As a species we owe our very existence to fear

But unreasoning fear is a problem. Excessive over-worrying will debilitate you.

But let's not think that the goal of life should be to live a worry-free, stress-free, fear-free existence.

Big mistake.

In fact, it's not only a mistake.

It's ridiculous.

We were not wired that way.

If we were we would end up like Bob. Dead.

Nerves are normal. So is a degree of anxiety.

Our goal is not to achieve a zen-like state of calm, living a care-free existence, walking through the meadows picking flowers whilst listening to the sounds of the ocean on our iPods. Not for most of us, anyway.

Trust me – that's not what we were designed to do.

That's not what makes us tick.

But neither were we meant to live life as an extreme version of Frank.

He did have some important stuff to be fearful about. Every day for Frank was a battle for survival. He owed his continuing existence to his ability to spot trouble and deal with it.

Fear was his friend.

There's a part of Frank's brain that we also have. In fact it's often referred to as our 'Primitive brain'. It's the first part of the child's brain to develop in the womb.

Its primary aim?

To keep you alive.

And it's bestowed on you a useful life-saving mechanism which you will have probably have heard of.

It's called your fight-or-flight response. So when we perceive a threat we can go into either fight mode where our body prepares itself for some form of combative action, or flight mode where we literally flee or withdraw from a situation. This explains why, if you think your house is being robbed whilst you're still at home (a threat), your first thought is not to reach for the aroma-therapy oils and run a hot bath. You either confront the intruder or plan a quick escape.

Unfortunately, Bob seemed to have a problem with his fight-or-flight response. Must have been part of a faulty batch. That's why we know we're not Bob's descendants.

But there is a problem with this evolutionary gift of ours. Despite all our modern sophistication, our designer lifestyles, our universities, deep down we still have our inner caveman as our constant companion. Frank lives on within us. You may feel more comfortable calling them Francesca, but either way they're still imprinted within our genetic code.

But it's helping us deal with a world that is somewhat different to Frank and Francesca's. Battling through rush-hour traffic rather than for survival is now the norm for most of us. And for some people dealing with a traffic warden is their equivalent to an encounter with a sabre-toothed tiger. (Although to be fair sabre-toothed tigers probably weren't as aggressive. Hey, just kidding.)

The problem is we still sometimes react to day-to-day hassles in the same way Frank and Francesca dealt with life-and-death issues on the savannah.

Our fight-or-flight response has become the equivalent of an internal smoke alarm inside our brain.

It's good to have a smoke alarm.

It can save your life.

But they can be oversensitive. A slightly overcooked piece of toast triggers the alarm in the same way as a smoke-filled room does. The principle of a smoke alarm is fine. It can be a life saver. But in practice it can also cause problems.

Likewise the principle of our internal fight-or-flight response is fine. To feel fear is fine.

Sometimes.

We need that adrenalin rush.

It helps us not only survive but thrive.

That's a good thing.

Like the smoke alarm.

But now in our modern 21st-century, fast-paced life our fight-or-flight response is being continually triggered.

Over minor, insignificant issues.

Over trivia.

Over events that haven't even happened yet.

Over traffic wardens, not sabre-toothed tigers.

Our world has become full of slightly overcooked toast, but our internal alarm is telling us our house is on fire.

That's what happens when our internal wiring is faulty.

Rather than equip us for life it disables us.

That's our challenge.

Worry can work.

It can keep us focused. It can prepare us for challenges.

But it can weaken us as well. Particularly when our wiring is faulty. And sometimes we react without engaging rational brain. When we do we may overreact and perhaps do something stupid. I should know. I've been there.

Let me share a personal experience with you.

I guess if I had to give a title to this story I would call it 'Helen and the slugs'. Sounds a little like the name of a punk band from the 1970s, but it illustrates how our primitive brain in its quest to protect us can sometimes jump to wrong conclusions.

Here's what happened.

It was late on one summer's evening. It was still warm but then sun had now set.

Darkness was now on duty.

Helen stepped out of the back door onto the patio as she desperately sought to retrieve the last Malteser from a bag I had mistakenly thrown away earlier.

I heard a loud scream.

My first thought was that she couldn't locate the Malteser bag.

I was wrong.

'We're being invaded by slugs.'

'Slugs? Are you sure?' was my rather bemused reply.

'There are hundreds of them; they're just outside the back door. They're heading towards us. They'll be in the kitchen before you know it.'

As far as I was aware Helen had not been drinking that evening. Chocolate was her only vice that night and I was fairly convinced that hadn't affected her eyesight.

Now I appreciate this wasn't exactly an encounter with a sabre-toothed tiger on the savannah, but Helen was clearly alarmed and I quickly bought into her state of panic.

'Are you sure they're slugs?'

'Absolutely. Take a look.'

I tentatively opened the door. I know it sounds stupid but I was slightly anxious. Although my imagination hadn't quite conjured up images of a giant slug, the thought of a few hundred seeking to invade our home was definitely disconcerting.

To be honest it was difficult to tell in the dark exactly what was on the patio area, but the word 'slug' had already been planted in my mind and I didn't feel calm or rational enough to conduct a thorough analysis of the creatures that lay before me.

I know this next bit will sound cruel.

I appreciate it may lead to a series of protests and calls for the public to boycott my books, but I need to tell it as it is.

We didn't have any slug pellets to hand. I know they can add a little colour and texture to a salad, but we'd gone with radishes instead.

'Salt will sort them,' I thought.

Helen agreed.

Salt seemed to be our only help.

Helen grabbed a tube of the best salt in the house.

In fact it was the only salt we had.

Flinging open the kitchen door she sprang into action like an elite member of a special forces unit embarking upon a raid into enemy territory.

Boy did she spread that salt.

The slugs had no chance.

Our survival was ensured.

Salt had saved the day.

It was either fight or flight.

Flee our home and leave it at the mercy of a marauding army of evil slugs.

Or stand and fight.

We had chosen the latter.

The rush of adrenalin we experienced made us feel good.

Our children were safe.

The next morning we returned to the scene of our triumph.

There were no slugs.

Not even dead ones.

There were, however, hundreds of small, slightly slug-shaped leaves on our patio.

I guess that's the problem with our primitive brain. It's wired to protect us from threats. But sometimes we react to imaginary threats: situations that we perceived to be a problem but actually weren't. We go into panic mode when there's nothing to panic about.

This story has an amusing and, for Helen and I, a rather embarrassing ending. But for some people their overactive imagination and over sensitive primitive brain means a life often lacking in peace of mind. That's a challenge. But a greater understanding of why we act and react the way we do can be the first step to helping us deal more effectively with our worries.

So let's take some time now to explore our brain in more detail and in doing so understand why it seems we're wired to worry. This will also reveal why being told to 'stop worrying' and 'use your common sense' is actually a lot harder than it sounds.

A bit about your brain

Let me introduce you to something you're well acquainted with, couldn't do without but rarely acknowledge – your brain. Your brain has evolved over thousands of years. If you were to weigh it (and personally I don't suggest you try) it won't do much harm to the scales, coming in at approximately 3 lb or 1.4 kg.

Without it we're dead.

Literally.

But have you ever taken time out to consider how this amazing piece of apparatus works? And in what ways could it actually contribute to your anxiety and stress levels unless you learn to understand it more?

Right then, let's take a brief tour of the brain. If you happen to be a neurologist or brain surgeon you may find this overview rather simplified and lacking in sufficient detail to help you conduct your next operation. That's absolutely fine. I can live with that. My goal is to simplify the complex, so here goes.

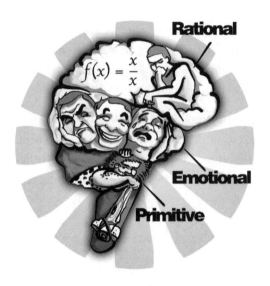

Let's begin our tour with:

1. **The primitive brain.** We've referred to this bit of your
   brain on several occasions so far. So here's a recap. This is
   the first part of the brain to develop in the mother's womb.
   Its goal is quite simple. It wants to keep you alive. It controls
   a range of functions, including your fight-or-flight response
   (which you should now be well acquainted with), your desire
   for food and your sex drive. It operates on an unconscious
   automatic level. It doesn't need any interference from you.
   It's been around a long time, thank you very much, and
   is quite happy to be left alone to get on with what it does
   best – keeping you alive. We owe our very existence as a
   species to this part of the brain. It's also something we share
   in common with much of the rest of the animal kingdom.

OK, now onto the next part.

2. **The emotional brain.** This is part of the limbic system and developed after the primitive part of the brain, but it's hardly the new kid on the block – it's been around for thousands of years. This is the part of the brain working in partnership with its close brother, 'primitive brain', that releases hormones such as cortisol and adrenalin into your system and can lead to you feeling energized, excited, anxious and fearful.

And finally,

3. **The rational brain.** Also known as the higher brain or neocortex (if you want to impress your friends). This really is the new kid in town in evolutionary terms. Rather than being a close brother to primitive and emotional brains it's more of a distant cousin. It's a more recent addition to the family in terms of our evolutionary development and not something we have in common with much of the rest of the animal kingdom. It's what in particular makes us unique as a species.

But there's a problem. It's not always on the best of terms with its cousins. In terms of age it's the youngest and that also leads to it not being able to exert the same influence and control as its more elderly and long-established relatives a lot of the time.

How our three brains operate under pressure

Let's be clear: the brain rarely if ever conducts a board meeting or a family conference. During a time of crisis the primitive brain doesn't think to check out its plans with rational brain before taking action. Decisions are not automatically deferred to rational brain. In fact it's often excluded from the process. Its own opinions count for very little when compared with the family heavyweights, primitive and emotional.

Emotional brain isn't checking out with rational brain about the intensity of its feelings. And primitive brain isn't particularly bothered about rational's view on the situation and whether it's being a little oversensitive to a possible threat.

Here's the real truth:

> Rational brain, despite its many attributes, rarely rules in a crisis

Any time the rational part of your brain does seem to be in control, just remember this. It's not permanent. Never take its influence for granted. Don't start thinking rational brain can start moving into a role with the title 'The Boss'. They won't achieve such status. Primitive and emotional brain have seen to that – or for the next few thousand years anyway. Influence is the most it can hope for, at least for the time being.

It's this relationship between the three brains that goes a long way to explaining why we don't always act as logically and rationally as we'd expect when under pressure. Remember the slug story? What were we thinking? Actually, we weren't thinking. We were reacting. We were in fight-or-flight mode. Stress can make you stupid, and when rational brain has been kept out of the decision-making process that's why we have to work hard to ensure rational brain does exert its influence.

Now when things are running smoothly primitive brain can take a short nap, but always with one eye open. It's always monitoring our environment. It's never in a deep sleep. It's the complete opposite in nature to a teenager in terms of its sleeping habits. You don't have to coax and counsel it from its place of rest with threats of wet flannels or sunlight.

Far from it.

Primitive brain is so on the ball that when it senses a threat it has sprung into action, ably assisted by emotional brain, before rational brain has got a clue what's happened.

Here's the real truth:

In terms of a potential threat our brains are wired to act first, think later

Spend too much time thinking and you could soon end up as dead meat as far as primitive and emotional brain are concerned. Hence no board meetings or family conferences. There's simply no time, and anyway, what would be the point? As far as primitive brain is concerned survival is not a duty to delegate. Ever.

And that's exactly the type of brain you would want to be in charge when on the African savannah fighting for survival. The only trouble is the environment and context in which primitive brain evolved is an entirely different one to the one it finds itself in now. But because our survival is still its primary concern, don't expect the fact that sabre-toothed tigers have taken a ticket to oblivion means primitive can relax.

It won't relax.

Ever.

So there's our problem. As mentioned earlier, our brains simply weren't developed to deal with life in the 21st century. And although rational brain has now taken to the stage it's not easy to get the spotlight away from its primitive and emotional cousins. Despite all its good intentions, our primitive and emotional brain can end up being the source of our stress and anxiety problems.

Yet when questioned, their defence would simply be this:

'Hey, we were just doing our job.'

That's why we often make snap decisions about people and situations. We act without thinking and can jump to conclusions without all the facts. Primitive and emotional brain don't wait for all the data to be analyzed before making a decision.

There just isn't the time.

Their underlying stance is 'It's better to be wrong but alive than to be certain of all your facts and dead.'

To be fair, you can't blame them for being this way, can you?

And you won't change it.

So what's the best you can hope for?

Three things.

You can learn to be more **aware** of primitive and emotional brain's role and impact.

Accept they're just doing their job.

Avoid allowing them to have complete control and a monopoly on how you behave.

Rational brain may be new in town and have to shout louder to be heard, but it's essential that we do hear its voice.

Here's the real truth:

> If we don't engage rational brain more often we might as well go back to our caves and hunt woolly mammoths

So make sure you take note of the insights and ideas we'll be exploring in Chapter 5, 'Let's Get Rational'. OK?

Why keeping perspective can be difficult to do

So what else is it about our brains that causes us to act irrationally and fail to engage our rational brain? Let's explore how our emotions impact our outlook on life and how we deal with challenging situations.

See if you can relate to the following.

Have you ever found yourself listening to a friend or colleague's problem and seen an obvious solution that they seem blind to?

Or listened with mild amusement to their issue and wondered what on earth all the fuss is about?

If so, you've just experienced the effects of the connection between rational perspective and emotional involvement. In a nutshell, the higher your emotional involvement in situation the harder it is to maintain a rational perspective. The graph below illustrates the point:

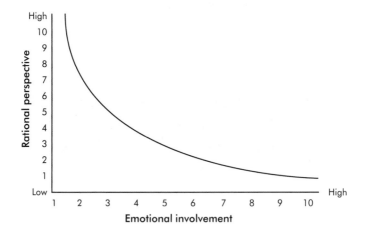

Now the above graph is an illustration of the potential challenges we face when emotionally involved in a situation. It's not a universal decree that we will never be able to think rationally when our emotional involvement is high – but it is saying it could be difficult. Let me elaborate.

Imagine the following scenario.

You bump into a casual acquaintance whilst out shopping. You make polite conversation and ask about them and their family. They seem a little harassed and anxious. They explain that their son, having secured a place at university, may, due to an admin error, have lost out on a place in the halls of residence. Such a calamity may now result in him having to share a house off campus with other students.

They look anxious as they update you on this breaking news.

But how are you feeling?

Go on, be honest.

Is it possible you'd be wondering why on earth they're so concerned? Are you likely to offer reassuring words of comfort along the lines of 'I'm sure everything will work out and maybe it's for the best.'

Go on, admit it, you would wouldn't you?

I certainly would.

Maybe you're thinking that they're guilty of making a mountain out of a molehill.

And guess what?

You'd be right.

You see, this is a classic example of two people discussing the same issue from two completely different places of emotional involvement. And as a result, their ability to see the situation from a rational perspective is completely different. Whilst one person allows a small issue to dominate their thinking and needs time to get things off their chest, the other one is thinking 'build a bridge, get over it.'

Here's another example.

You're at a party and a good friend of your partner's appears to ignore them. Your partner is hurt. They feel rejected now. Rejection is a powerful and strong emotion. It affects their whole evening. The point is, you don't see it as a big deal. You weren't the one who felt rejected. You're enjoying yourself with your friends. You make the unforgiveable mistake of making a joke out of the whole situation. Big mistake.

And as a result of your rational, detached but perhaps also slightly insensitive response, you quickly see the likelihood of a relaxed and enjoyable evening with your partner evaporate into thin air.

You see, that's how our emotions can affect us. We lose perspective. Primitive and emotional brain have taken over. That's not wrong necessarily, but here's the real truth:

When we're highly emotional we lose perspective and the ability to easily access solutions to our problems

We worry rather than work through our concerns logically.

It's like all roads leading to the rational part of your brain have been closed for major repairs and there's no sign of a diversion. Or at least it seems that way to you.

Those around you seem skilled at finding an alternative route. If their emotional involvement is low, then seeing a way forward is potentially far easier.

It's like one person driving in torrential rain on the motorway with only one windscreen wiper working, compared to someone else driving on a bright clear day. And that's why one person's worries barely register on someone else's radar. It's why one person sees solutions screaming for attention whilst another stumbles along in the dark.

That's the impact of your emotional brain. And when you see how its close brother primitive brain also works, then we can rightly argue that we are in fact wired to worry. We're certainly predisposed to being this way.

However, despite this fact, as we saw from Chapter 2 other factors also influence how we respond to situations. And despite our wiring we can learn to manage our primitive and emotional responses more effectively. But when we don't it does have consequences. As we're about to see in our next chapter.

Before we do, however, let's just take a moment for some reflection.

Hammock time

- Can you think of any examples in your life, perhaps from the last few weeks, where primitive and emotional brain caused you to jump to conclusions or overreact to a situation?
- How might someone who was less emotionally involved have responded to the same situation?
- If you had the same experience, knowing what you now know, would you respond differently next time? If so, in what way?
- What would you say has been your main insight from this chapter?

Chapter 4

Ever Got Lost in Loopy Logic?

We're now on our final chapter in helping us to stop and understand some of the causes and reasons why we worry. You're about to discover the impact of not using your rational brain to address your worries logically as we explore some alternative strategies that people use to deal with their worries. Once we understand what doesn't work and the reasons why, we'll hopefully stop wasting our time and energy on these ineffective strategies.

When my daughter Ruth was younger she developed a fear of sharks. Nothing wrong about that, you may say. Sharks can be scary creatures and they come with a fearsome reputation – perhaps wrongly so, but they do. However, Ruth's concern was that she might encounter sharks not in the sea but at the local swimming pool. Well, the swimming pools of Warrington may be famous for many things, but sharks aren't one of them.

Ruth's concern was not logical. But it was real. As I can testify from taking her swimming and remembering her genuine concern. She's OK now, just in case you're wondering. Although she does insist on wearing a reinforced chainmail swimsuit and being lowered into the pool in a cage.

You may read about Ruth's irrational fears and smile. She was just a kid, after all. Children have all sorts of irrational fears, don't they? But not you. You're mature. You're an adult. You would never be so irrational about stuff that happens in your life.

Would you?

Really?

Is that always the case? Or are we sometimes living life with the mind of a child in an adult's body?

Psychologists Cary Morewedge from Carnegie Mellon University and Michael Norton from Harvard University carried out an experiment to ascertain whether our modern minds are attracted to the notion that dreams can predict the future. ('When dreaming is believing: The (motivated) interpretation of dreams', *Journal of Personality and Social Psychology* **96**, 249–64, 2009).

Around 180 commuters were given the following scenario: Imagine that you've booked to be on a certain flight but the day before you were due to fly out one of four events occurred:

1   The government issued a warning raising the national threat level of a terrorist attack.

2   They thought about their plane crashing on the flight they planned to take.

3   They dreamt about their plane crashing on the flight they planned to take.

4   A real plane crash occurred on the same route that they were flying.

After imagining each scenario, people were then asked to rate the likelihood of them cancelling their flight.

So what would you have as top of your list?

Well you may be interested to learn that in this particular piece of research it was the third option, dreaming about an accident, that was deemed most likely to cause people to cancel their flight.

So these people put the influence of a dream as having a more significant impact on their future actions than a government warning or an actual plane crash.

Strange?

Not really.

People are actually quite skilled at adopting what I refer to as 'loopy logic' in terms of how they see the world and deal with problems. And just to clarify, I use the term 'loopy' to mean 'strange, not acting normally, crazy', as in 'the guy was a bit loopy'.

As we've seen from the previous chapter, primitive and emotional brain are very skilled at relegating rational brain to the subs bench in some cases. This in turn can lead to all kinds of irrational thinking that causes people to worry and stress about a whole variety of weird and wonderful things. And this lack of rational, logical thinking begins in our childhood, the story of my daughter being one example of that. But it seems for some people there are no signs of it fading into the background as they get older. Despite their maturity in age their brain can still operate like an adolescent's.

Can you relate to that at all?

Perhaps you've looked back on some of your past decisions and actions and thought 'What was I thinking?' or 'Why on earth did I worry?'

I certainly have.

And sometimes we worry about the trivial stuff but don't get concerned about the important stuff. Bizarre, eh? But the real truth is this:

Loopy logic inevitably leads to loopy behaviour

Nine symptoms of suffering from loopy logic

Let's examine how loopy logic leads to loopy behaviour when we allow primitive and emotional brain to deal with worry without the help of rational brain. See which ones you've ever experienced.

1. Feeding your fears

It seems some people's way of dealing with fear and anxiety is to feast on more of it.

Worried about crime?

Read more about it.

Watch TV programmes that give graphic details about victims. Read the stories. Download the podcasts or watch the television.

Some people are hooked on CNN – Constant Negative News.

They actually look for reasons to justify their fear.

Psychologists call this 'confirmation bias', whereby we actively seek out information to confirm our view of the world. If we're looking for the terrible and the tragic we'll find it. If we're looking for a reason to feel fearful about our future we'll find it. It's like we're on a constant quest to justify our worries. And in doing so we increase our own fears.

Logical?

Of course not.

This consumption of the so-called 'facts' unduly heightens people's awareness and sensitivity to possible threats no matter how rare or unlikely they may be – which, if we're trying to worry less, is the equivalent of trying to lose weight by embarking on a high-fat, high-calorie diet. It just doesn't make sense. Agree? But that doesn't stop us doing it.

2. Avoiding your issues

This is an approach favoured particularly by male members of the population. If I avoid thinking and talking about my worries they will disappear. It's a bit like during my speaking events when I announce I will be choosing a couple of volunteers to help me illustrate a point. Immediately I become aware that people start to avoid eye contact with me and develop a deep interest in their fingernails or the colour of the carpets. Almost as if to say 'If I can't see you then you can't see me!'

It's bizarre.

But people do it.

In fact, I've done it.

Harmless really.

But avoiding important issues and dismissing them from your mind is not harmless. Such an approach could actually be inflicting long-term harm.

Here's the real truth:

> By avoiding the problem you're actually allowing it to escalate

Got money worries?

Well, avoiding the issue makes it worse. Much worse.

(OK, now if you have a phobia I can understand why you avoid certain situations, and if that's the case you may need professional help. But I'm talking about everyday worries, not phobias.)

So if you're avoiding your problems and that doesn't concern you, fine. That's your choice. But be clear on this. It will more than likely worry someone close to you. Not great for them is it?

Maybe it's time to ditch this form of loopy logic and face up to your problems. For your sake. And probably for other people's sake too.

3. Playing the victim role

Some people have developed a persecution complex in terms of how they see themselves. They believe life is actually out to get them and that they're powerless to resist such an assault. Problems pile up around them but they believe it's through no fault of their own.

Their anxiety and stress is born from a belief that they have no control or influence as to what happens to them.

Woes and worries seem to be poured upon them from above and they struggle to find a place to shelter.

This loopy logic turns into a self-fulfilling prophecy. Because they play the role of victim and therefore don't even try to help themselves, people fail to develop the necessary coping skills to deal with life's challenges and so their problems increase. Fate has dealt them a bad hand it would seem and they're unaware they can open a new deck.

4. Using worry as witchcraft

OK, the word witchcraft may seem a little dramatic, but some people's loopy logic convinces them that merely the act of worrying will in some magical and mystical way resolve their problems. (Remember that story of the man who threw paper on the rail track to keep away elephants?) In fact they worry that if they don't worry then something bad will happen! Now I'm fairly sure this is done at a subconscious rather than conscious level, but why would someone persist with such bizarre beliefs?

Well, think about it for a moment.

If I worry about something happening, such as one of my children being injured at school, and it doesn't happen, then in some mysterious way maybe my worry worked.

Strange, eh? To think the actual process of worrying will in some way cast a spell to achieve a particular outcome. Sounds a bit loopy to me. And perhaps not one that many people will admit to.

But it happens. In fact it's akin to 'tempting fate,' whereby because you said something positive will happen you're now concerned something negative will occur instead. Worry as witchcraft works the opposite way. By worrying about a negative outcome happening we hope it will actually lead to something positive occurring.

5. Wearing worry as an identity

We're very good at labelling ourselves and others. It makes life easier when we can pigeonhole people. But how useful is it to give ourselves a negative label?

Perhaps we convince ourselves that the labels can't be changed. Elements of a victim mentality seep into our thinking.

'I'm a worrier.' And underneath this declaration written in small print is '… and there's nothing I can do about it.'

Perhaps if we unpacked the phrase 'worrier' and elaborated on it more we'd be less likely to wear it.

'I'm a worrier. I waste time and energy mentally torturing myself about issues, problems and people. The majority of what I worry about rarely happens anyway, and deep down I realize worry is worthless if it doesn't in some way motivate me to take action. I'm also aware that life is an amazing privilege and yet, by my own self-imposed weird way of thinking, I actually rob myself of enjoying and appreciating many of its great pleasures.'

OK, I confess it would be a rather large label, but you get my point.

How many people would really want to wear it?

But they're quite happy wearing the condensed version.

Loopy, eh?

Here's the real truth:

A change in identity can lead to a change in behaviour

Maybe it's time to lose the 'I'm a worrier' label. What do you reckon?

6. Just thinking happy thoughts

This is a different kind of loopy logic. In fact it's the complete opposite of worry in many ways and is a subtle form of avoidance. In a nutshell, if I think happy thoughts then nothing bad will happen.

Actually, that doesn't sound too bad does it?

Certainly better than worrying all the time about stuff that rarely, if ever, happens.

Well, you're right.

To a point.

Having an optimistic view on life is helpful.

But if you're faced with some real challenges then optimism may be nothing more than false hope.

And hope is not a strategy.

Optimism may make you feel better in the short-term, but it's not doing anything concrete to help you deal with the situation if it doesn't lead to you taking action.

When I recently lay on an operating table whilst under local anaesthetic I did in fact think happy thoughts.

It was a welcome distraction.

It took my mind off a procedure in which there was nothing I could do to influence the outcome other than keep still.

Let me assure you, thinking happy thoughts did help.

On that occasion.

But it's not a strategy I'm going to regularly call upon to deal with life's challenges.

The delusion of happy thinking may in fact be a smokescreen that hides our indecisiveness and unwillingness to confront issues.

The American speaker Jim Rohn brilliantly illustrated why optimism is not enough with the following example.

If you're out sailing and the wind changes direction, the pessimist says, 'That's awful, what are we going to do?'

The optimist just has happy thoughts and says, 'Never mind, the wind will change direction again I'm sure.'

But the leader adjusts the sails.

Thinking happy thoughts when there is absolutely nothing you can do to help influence or improve a situation is fine.

Having it as part of your general overall approach to life is acceptable.

But having it as your single most important strategy in dealing with issues is crazy.

In fact it's loopy.

Here's an example of when I illustrated why positive or happy thinking alone is not enough to deal with our challenges. I did the following exercise on one of my Presentation Masterclasses.

I lit a candle and asked the delegates to focus on the flame.

Our goal was to extinguish the flame by simply using the power of our thoughts.

We were playing a version of happy thinking, with the emphasis being on believing our positive thoughts would exert an invisible force that would result in the flame going out.

The delegates were a little dubious.

And with good reason.

But I convinced them I was being deadly serious.

I switched the lights out and we stood up with each person concentrating on willing the flame to go out by purely the power of their thoughts.

With twenty people in the same room that meant a lot of positive energy was being directed towards that candle.

We waited.

And we focused.

We waited some more.

The room was silent.

We were all transfixed on the flame.

And then after two minutes

nothing had happened.

I moved forward.

I blew out the flame.

The group looked a little shocked.

'Well,' I announced, 'It just goes to show – positive thinking is not enough. You have to take action.'

The real truth is:

> When you're confronted with challenges, life rewards positive action, not positive thinking.

Happy thinking alone is not enough.

False optimism is dangerous. Especially when you convince yourself that bad things happen to other people but never to you. Psychologists call this the 'myth of personal invulnerability', whereby some people persistently underestimate their susceptibility to life crises and therefore have more difficulty adjusting to them should they occur. The reality is that if you go through life not expecting to deal with the crises which the average person has to contend with, you are more likely to cope poorly when they do occur. That's why false optimism is dangerous and why happy thinking deludes us into a false sense of security.

Here's the deal. The universe will not magically transform your situation because you decide to abdicate personal responsibility and just be happy. And if you can think of an example when that did happen, then you got lucky.

Congratulations.

My guess is, someone else bailed you out.

This time.

But to believe that will always be the case in the future is stupid.

Deep down you know that's another example of loopy logic.

Trust me: you'll feel a lot better about yourself and life when you learn to blow out your own candles.

7. Giving power to 'things' and dates

I once gave 23 radio interviews over a 24-hour period. I remember the dates well. My first interview was at 7pm on Thursday 12 May and during that evening and throughout the next day I spoke about 'Yippee, it's Friday 13th'. The media was fascinated by advice that it was up to us to make this day the luckiest not the unluckiest day of the year.

I must confess I'm amazed by both the creativity and stupidity of the human race. Imagine coming up with a special day and date that was deemed to be unlucky? And imagine people being daft enough to believe that bad things happened to them specifically because it was that day.

Crazy, eh?

But never underestimate so-called rational, intelligent people's ability to think and do irrational things. Remember how persuasive primitive and emotional brain can be.

And yet strangely there will be people arguing vehemently that Friday 13th is an unlucky day. In fact they'll have evidence to prove it.

Well ask several million people if they've had anything go wrong on a specific day and, guess what?

You'll find your evidence.

Mind you, ask several million people if they've had anything go right on a specific date and equally you'll find evidence to support the notion that that was a lucky day.

Such a phenomenon is simply down to a law. The law of large numbers. As laws go the title seems fairly self-explanatory.

Work with a big enough group of people and you're sure to find two or three examples to support whatever case you're putting forward. And then, of course, conveniently ignore the rest who had a fairly mundane Friday 13th. The fact is that many of us are more susceptible to persuasion by an anecdote than by hard data. It appeals more to our emotional brain.

And maybe it's another subtle or sophisticated way of abdicating responsibility.

Maybe we find it quite exciting to put our destiny in something that is beyond our control.

And if you're superstitious and having a rabbit's foot makes you feel lucky (although it didn't do much for the rabbit) then that's your choice. That's fairly harmless.

But if you start to give your superstitions a certain power then you do need to be careful.

Here's the deal.

Trouble does not come in threes.

A broken mirror does not mean seven years of bad luck.

And chill out if your clover only has three leaves.

In fact, if you want things to go well perhaps you don't need to 'touch wood' but 'tap into your brain' a little more.

You see, when we give power to things and dates, no matter how tenuously so, we stop looking to ourselves for answers. We subtly disempower ourselves. It's like being in the driver's seat but with your hands off the steering wheel. It's not the greatest strategy for helping you get to where you want to be.

And next time you find yourself saying 'I'm a great believer in fate', is that actually a glorified way of saying you're conveniently abdicating personal responsibility?

Is it?

Is that what you're really saying?

Honestly?

Have your fun with dates and superstitions by all means, but make sure that's all it is.

Otherwise you've just bought into another form of loopy logic.

8. Worrying about the past

Actually there's not a lot we need to say about this point. It's been summed up in a phrase that seems to have been passed on through the generations;

'Don't cry over spilt milk.'

It's one of those phrases that logically we embrace but in reality we find difficult to apply. Clearly part of the healing process involves reliving and retelling the past, but make sure you're careful how long it lasts and how many people you tell.

You cannot manage history.

You can learn from your past.

You can learn from your mistakes.

But you can't change your past. No amount of worrying will ever do that.

You can only change how it's impacting your present. Dwelling on past pains and regrets weakens you. It makes you more prone to anxiety and stress. It robs you of the ability to move on.

It's time to start a new chapter.

And remember your story may have had difficult and even painful times but you're still the writer of the rest of your script. (We'll explore this more a little later.)

Perhaps it really is time to let go of stuff you can no longer do anything about.

Learn from it.

Be better because of it.

Now let go

and

move on.

Easier said than done, I know. But hang on in there, because you will discover ideas later that will help you to do so. It might not be easy, but it is possible. Promise.

9. Paralysis by analysis

Ever wrestled over a decision?

Ever worried that you may be about to do something you'll later regret?

Ever embarked upon a self-torture programme by continually asking yourself 'What if?' followed by 'Are you sure you're doing the right thing? Are you certain?'

Well, have you?

I certainly have.

Although perhaps not to the degree that I used to and not to the degree that some people do.

You see, unlike a game of heads and tails, most decisions in life are not clear cut. Most things are not either right or wrong. And because of this fact questions can race through our mind over issues ranging from the major to the mundane.

Should we move house?

Is it time for a new car?

Should I book my holiday late or early?

Should I ask that person out on a date?

Yet despite things being rarely clear cut we often place ourselves under unnecessary pressure as we pursue the holy grail marked 'the right answer.'

We wrestle with uncertainty, desperately wanting life to scream out with clarity the path we should take.

And we worry when it doesn't.

Are we moving house at the right time? What if house prices fall? Will I be able to afford the mortgage payments? What if I lose my job? What if we regret not moving?

It's like we're in our own personal game show, where we get to be both the quiz master and the contestant and yet we're still not sure of the answers.

And the reason?

We hate the thought of looking stupid. We struggle with the fear of loss compared to the joy of gain.

But reality rules. And even though we can make some educated guesses based on as much research as possible, life does not come with a set of guarantees.

That makes us uncomfortable.

We like certainty.

Some people crave it.

We're wary of the unknown.

That's understandable.

Living in a state of constant uncertainty and being cool about it would make you the exception, not the rule.

But uncertainty comes with the territory.

Fact.

But some people ignore the facts. They believe they have to be in control.

About most things. Most of the time.

And if they're not they feel way out of their comfort zone.

Anxious. Stressed.

Fear is not their friend anymore. It's become their enemy.

It knocks constantly on the door of their mind with unanswerable questions.

And we delude ourselves with thinking if I just delay my decision a little longer the perfect solution will appear.

And we wait

and wait

and

wait

until

it

comes.

And then worry when it doesn't.

Our confidence drains as our anxiety increases.

But here's the real truth:

> There's rarely ever a perfect time.
> Or a perfect decision

There are maybe better times to do something and there may be better decisions that could have been made, but the pursuit of perfection can often be pointless.

Live with it.

Set a time limit for your decision.

Get as many facts as you can.

Seek advice.

Weigh up what people say.

Then act.

Do something.

Anything.

Just break out of paralysis by analysis.

You're not a psychic.

You can make intelligent predictions about the future and you can increase your odds of success.

But you can't make perfect predictions.

None of us can.

So get over it.

Live with it.

And let go of loopy logic.

The real truth is:

Action brings satisfaction. OK?

Right, so we've explored nine types of loopy logic. Just before we reflect on them, let's briefly explore a behaviour that some people describe as one of their main strategies in dealing with worry, whilst others may see it as just another example of loopy logic. I wonder where you stand?

Is praying a little bit loopy?

I was asked recently if I saw prayer as another form of loopy logic and perhaps as a subtle way of abdicating personal responsibility when faced with a problem. Before I answer that, let me acknowledge that prayer can mean different things to different people and can be a very personal and private matter. I write in the context of being exposed to the experience of prayer within a Christian tradition, but I recognize other people's experiences may be significantly different to my own. However, as prayer is a way in which people deal with worry, I want to share briefly a few of my thoughts on what some people regard as an important topic.

In terms of prayer being seen as loopy logic, well, a lot could depend on the person's *beliefs* about prayer rather than the act of praying itself. If someone believes there is a bearded man in the sky who's a cross between Father Christmas and a giant puppeteer whose sole role in life is to sort out their problems whilst they sit back and do nothing, then I have sympathy with those who see prayer as a form of loopy logic.

However, the people I know who pray (and I'll happily admit I'd be one of them) would strongly reject such a narrow interpretation or outlook on prayer. There's perhaps a lot more to the subject than purely seeing 'God' or whatever term you use to describe the person or being you're praying to, as the 'guy in the sky who helps me get by'.

But here's why I think that for a number of practical reasons prayer can be beneficial in helping some people deal with their worries, whether they're religious or not.

First, the very act of speaking out your concerns by praying can itself bring a sense of clarity to the person praying. Prayer encourages us to articulate our thoughts and feelings, which up until that point we may have failed to do. It can help unravel our own tangled thinking on an issue. Also there's an unspoken expectation that you're not going to be interrupted when you're praying, unlike perhaps when talking things through with a friend. I guess you're not expecting to be contradicted, challenged or questioned further about your issues during your prayer time in the way you might be when talking to someone else.

Prayer, it would seem, can give people the space and the airtime to offload their concerns without interruption; a luxury not always found in our interactions with others where people are often quick to offer advice and reassurance without perhaps meeting our real need just to be heard.

In a sense the person praying may believe they're being listened to unconditionally and without judgement, something they feel might be difficult to achieve outside the context of prayer.

Also, for some people, prayer is a time for quiet reflection and contemplation – not a bad combination for someone who is feeling stressed and anxious. It can also be in the stillness that some idea, thought or inspiration may come to the person praying. Something that might not have occurred unless you were taking time out to pray.

Certain types of prayer also encourage people to practise thanksgiving, which is another way of expressing gratitude for life. Countless psychologists, including the father of the positive psychology movement, Martin Seligman, argue that expressing gratitude can have a profound benefit on our own emotional wellbeing. Perhaps another reason why people claim prayer is beneficial?

Ultimately, whether prayer works will continue to be open to debate. However, the key perhaps is whether *you believe it works*. If you do then this can influence whether you continue to worry about an issue or not. Belief in a higher being may encourage us to do all we can within our control to influence a situation (something we'll explore later in the book) whilst learning to accept and respect that some things cannot be influenced by ourselves. As the writer Larry Eisenberg said, 'For peace of mind we need to resign as general manager of the universe.'

So is it loopy to pray? Well, clearly it is to some people, especially to those who would never dream of doing so themselves. And to those who pray perhaps as a way of excusing themselves from taking any responsibility for their own issues, then there's a strong case to argue that it is loopy. But many people, whether religious or not, would testify to the importance of prayer in helping them worry less and enjoy life more.

I'll leave you to decide which camp you're in. (If you're interested in exploring in more detail why religious practices such as prayer may not be as loopy as the recent atheist literature represents them as being, then you may want to check out an article by A McGee, 'Is Dawkins a Modern-Day Nicodemus?', *Quadrant* LV, April 2011.)

Right, let's get back to looking at those nine symptoms of loopy logic.

So how loopy can you be?

My guess is a visitor from another planet would be incredibly impressed by what the human species has achieved so far. The amazing work of surgeons and scientists. The advances in technology. Our constant quest to explore and improve. To innovate and create.

Hey, as a member of the human race I think we deserve a pat on the back.

But I also think this same visitor from this other planet may also observe how we think and behave with both amusement and incredulity. The question they might ask is perhaps one we also need to ask ourselves:

How on earth do so-called rational, intelligent, successful people do such stupid things?

Look, I'm not calling you stupid. But let's be honest, as you review that list of examples of loopy logic are you guilty of at least some of them? Let's recap on that list and, as you do, be brutally honest about the ones you most relate to. (Remember our previous chapter gave us some big clues as to why we're not as rational as we'd like to think we are.)

	Always	Sometimes	Rarely	Never
Feeding your fears	☐	☐	☐	☐
Avoiding your issues	☐	☐	☐	☐
Playing the victim role	☐	☐	☐	☐
Using worry as witchcraft	☐	☐	☐	☐
Wearing worry as an identity	☐	☐	☐	☐
Just thinking happy thoughts	☐	☐	☐	☐
Giving power to things and dates	☐	☐	☐	☐
Worrying about the past	☐	☐	☐	☐
Paralysis by analysis	☐	☐	☐	☐

Hammock time

- Out of the nine symptoms, which ones particularly stood out for you?
- How do those symptoms impact your day-to-day life?
- Which symptoms would you say you experience less now than you did previously?
- Which symptoms have you seen in other people?
- If you had to choose one symptom that you want to address in particular, which would it be?
- What would be the consequences if you don't deal with that symptom?

Now if the only box you ticked for all nine symptoms was 'never', then I congratulate you. I guess my question would be what prompted you to read this book in the first place?

However, in the majority of cases most people relate to some of these symptoms – hence they have a problem with worry. Now in the case of 'just thinking happy thoughts', their actual problem with worry is they don't have an effective strategy for dealing with issues and pretend there are no problems. The happy demeanour they display may hide more deep-rooted problems. Sometimes it's only by expressing our concerns rather than hiding behind a mask that we're then able to deal with them. If you're guilty of this approach you have to be prepared to challenge yourself: 'Am I deluding myself that everything is OK when deep down I know it's not?'

As for the other symptoms, only you can decide if you've answered them honestly. If you have, then they will help you decide whether you've got a mild form of loopy logic or are suffering from a more acute case of it.

Either way, we need some ideas and maybe a little inspiration to help us out of this loopy logic maze, and that's exactly what the rest of this book is about.

Having taken time to stop and understand, we're now at the point where we're ready to move on to some solutions.

So make sure you're focused and ready to explore the next section, because we're going to look at a whole host of solutions, some obvious, some less so, that will help you to worry less and enjoy life more.

Section Two

Move On

Chapter 5

Let's Get Rational

$f(x) = \dfrac{x}{x}$

So far we've looked at why worry is a big deal. We've explored nine reasons why we worry and also learnt a little more about our primitive, emotional and rational brain. In our last chapter we examined the ways we sometimes get lost in loopy logic. Now, with all those ideas and insights out in the open, it's time to see in this chapter how we can move on to use our rational brain to help us deal more effectively with life's challenges. And although there are still plenty of ideas to discover, be prepared to expose your own worries to some scrutiny as we take time to explore some practical ways to deal with your worries.

TWO GREAT WAYS TO USE YOUR RATIONAL BRAIN

1. How to develop a Triple A strategy

So what's a Triple A strategy? Well, in this section we're going to raise our 'Awareness' surrounding our worries, then move on to some 'Analysis' of them before finally looking at some 'Actions' to address them. OK, let's get started with the first insight.

Awareness
Sometimes it's helpful simply to ask yourself 'What am I actually stressed, anxious or worried about?' With this question you'll find the following really helpful.

Is my worry related to a current situation I'm facing? Perhaps it's related to your health, a problem at work, some conflict at home or a bill that's just arrived this morning. If so this is sometimes referred to as **situational stress**. Your stress is related to a specific situation that is happening at the moment.

Alternatively, your concern may be regarding something that you are expecting to happen in the future. Perhaps it's an upcoming exam, a job interview, the results from a health examination or a presentation you have to make in the near future. As such the actual event or situation has yet to occur but your mind is focused on some future situation. This is often referred to as **anticipatory stress**. And although the issue has yet to take place, in reality it's already happening inside your head.

Now when that's the case your ever attentive primitive brain is triggered by the anticipation of this challenge and immediately prepares you to deal with it. Don't expect its message to be 'Hey, relax, this is weeks off yet. You've got plenty of time to prepare.' Primitive brain doesn't work like that. It wouldn't be doing its job if it did. That's what rational brain is for.

The real truth is:

> Your primitive brain cannot tell the difference between an actual event and a vividly imagined one

As a result, emotional brain also gets involved and you begin to experience feelings of anxiety about events and situations that might not actually occur.

Rough deal, eh?

But it's well worth raising your levels of awareness and asking yourself which type of stress are you currently experiencing – situational or anticipatory? The answer to this is may influence the action you take.

Now apologies, but I've got some bad news.

There's actually a third type of stress to be aware of. It's often known as **residual stress**. In other words it's the after-effects of a situation that has already occurred. In extreme cases this is known as post-traumatic stress. However, people can experience residual stress for a variety of reasons, two of which are at opposite ends of the spectrum.

One reason is due to the fact that we experience a particular event and then fail to talk about it or seek support from others. The approach of some people is to bottle up their worries and in doing so they find no outlet for the stress and anxiety building up within them. A bit like blowing up an already overinflated balloon, sometimes we pop over a seemingly trivial issue.

The rather dated and unhelpful view that people, particularly men, should keep a stiff upper lip contributes to this problem, as does the belief that it is wrong to show emotions. Whilst I'm not advocating that we wear our hearts on our sleeves and unburden our worries to the next person we meet in the street, I am saying we all need a release valve of some sort. What those release valves are we'll explore later.

Yet another cause for residual stress is for entirely the opposite reason. Some people have the habit of taking every opportunity to offload their stress but then fail to realize when enough is enough.

The real truth is:

> To re-tell is to re-live and that's not always helpful

Just because someone asks you how you are, that's not necessarily a mandate for you to tell them the entire history of your worries, challenges and setbacks. When you do, you're dredging up your pain or hurt once more. There's no need to be in denial, but neither is there a need to detail your issues at every opportunity.

Now it's over to you

So let's take some time out for you to think about the issues that concern you most. You can use the box below, download it from my website, www.theSUMOguy.com, or draw up your own. In completing it the aim is to help raise your awareness of whether your stress relates more to you current situation, anticipating a future event or challenge or focusing on something that is now in the past.

In completing the exercise, don't feel you have to come up with five worries. You may only have one or two particular concerns at the moment. However, you may want to reflect on the kind of issues that do cause you worry, anxiety and stress and decide which category they fall into. Life, however, is not always simple and straightforward, and it might be that certain issues you identify fall into more than one box. Either way it's still a helpful exercise in raising your awareness around your issues and it's possible that you might find some potential patterns emerging.

So start by writing down what you're worried, anxious or stressed about and then put a tick in the box or boxes marked situational, anticipatory and residual.

What I am worried, anxious or stressed about	Situational – it's happening now	Anticipatory – it may or may not happen	Residual – it's already happened
1.	☐	☐	☐
2.	☐	☐	☐
3.	☐	☐	☐
4.	☐	☐	☐
5.	☐	☐	☐

Notice any patterns emerging from doing the exercise?

Now let's explore the next insight in delivering our Triple A strategy.

Analysis

So having raised our awareness about the types of worry, anxiety and stress we're experiencing we're now going to dig a little deeper and look at their causes.

In analyzing our worries, the following questions will prove helpful in getting our issues into perspective and once again engaging the services of our rational brain. We're going to explore three reasons for your worries: historical, hysterical or helpful. The real truth is this:

> We need to deal with the root of our worries, not just the fruit of them

Let's start with the first one.

Historical
Memories and experiences from your past can be the reason you're experiencing anxiety in your present.

For instance, if you were mugged whilst once walking home late at night, your levels of anxiety if you find yourself in a similar situation of walking home alone would be potentially a lot higher than the person who has never been mugged. Similarly if you experienced heavy turbulence and a drop in cabin pressure on your first ever flight then this could affect how you feel about flying in the future.

On a perhaps more mundane level, if you went for a job interview and found the whole experience intimidating and nerve wracking then you're unlikely to welcome with open arms the opportunity to go through a similar ordeal again, particularly if you felt you didn't perform well at the interview. Likewise, if your mind goes blank during a presentation or your PowerPoint presentation freezes (although having seen many presentations that might not be a bad thing), your feelings of discomfort are likely to be high if you're called upon to do another one.

Whatever the situation, there are possibly good or certainly understandable reasons why an experience from the past still influences the way you feel about a particular event now.

Please note, however, that I used the word 'understandable,' not 'inevitable'. Your concerns, however, are not without some substance – there are some historical reasons.

The next one is interesting.

Hysterical

This is where you allow primitive and emotional brain off the leash whilst keeping rational brain firmly chained up in the corner cupboard, under heavy sedation. Your worries and concerns lack any real rhyme or reason except for some incredibly remote minuscule possibility. The noise you hear in the night could indeed be the footsteps of the mass murderer you believe could be currently operating in your area (and if indeed there is one then your fears are not hysterical), or perhaps one of the kids has just gone to the toilet. Yes, you could be struck by lightning whilst out walking in the rain, but that's hardly a reason to stay in the house hiding under the bed 'just in case'.

And although you may be feeling a little under the weather, this is perhaps not the time to say your last goodbyes and start checking the websites of your local funeral directors. And believing you may have contracted HIV Aids because you used a public toilet and forgot to disinfect the seat is taking things a little too far.

OK, I'm exaggerating my point.

To some extent.

But rumours circulate.

And the crazier they are the wider their circulation.

The internet has seen to that.

In fact, one website was set up to investigate the validity of such stories because of the ferocity at which they were being circulated and also believed. If you feel there's a good chance that you are likely to be murdered by an intruder, be struck by lightning and contact HIV Aids from a public toilet, then do check out www.snopes.com. It deals with a whole host of rumours and will do much to dampen down some hysterical thinking that on one level seems mildly amusing yet can actually be quite distressing in terms of our own mental wellbeing.

The question is, why on earth would rational, sane and sensible people be so influenced by weird and wacky stories? As we've already seen, primitive and emotional brain are strong factors in why this is the case. Let me also remind you of another reason we touched on earlier.

Maybe it's got something to do with how we were brought up.

You see, fear has been a weapon wielded by many parents in order to control their children's behaviour.

Have you ever come across any of the following statements?

- If you pull a face and the wind changes direction you'll stay that way.

- If you sit too close to the television you'll go blind.

- If you don't wash behind your ears potatoes will grow there.

- Picking your nose makes your nostrils bigger.

- If you're naughty Father Christmas won't bring you any presents.

- If you don't eat all your dinner you'll upset your favourite teddy.

If you can think of any more I'd love to hear from you. Please email Paul.McGee@theSUMOguy.com and they might well be included in the next edition of the book.

Clearly we're not here to play the blame game, but unintention-ally and inadvertently our family may have laid the foundations on which some people's bizarre beliefs are built. Not that you'd realize that as a four-year-old, however. But it seems old habits do indeed die hard, even when we're adults.

So here are a couple of great ways to help yourself when you're suffering from the hysterical habit:

1. **Do the maths**. Ask yourself 'OK, Paul (helpful if you use your own name, however), in all honesty how probable is that really?' Allow statistics to stun your worry. Do your research on what the odds are on the likelihood of what you're worrying about actually happening.

2. **Challenge your thinking**. Ask yourself 'How often do my dire predictions come true, really?' (If you can't quickly come up with six examples then just admit you're a lousy psychic.)

In effect you're being your own coach and challenger, and using your own name when asking the question increases this effect.

By doing so you're actually engaging your rational brain, which is no bad thing, as it's got a lot it can do to support you, and has more insight about certain situations than its oversensitive cousins primitive brain and emotional brain.

And remember, when you're feeling anxious about a particular issue, feelings are just feelings. They're not facts. Don't ignore your feelings, but don't make them the sole arbitrator and deter-mining factor in what you think about a situation. OK? That's really important to remember.

Trust me.

Now for the third reason for why you might worry.

The real truth is:

> Some worries are entirely legitimate and often helpful

Helpful

By now you've hopefully realized that I'm not suggesting that a worry-free existence is either achievable or desirable. If you live on a busy road and have small children, then being concerned about their safety sounds like a rather good idea. Having an important presentation to make for work should invoke enough concern that you want to prepare well. And if you do find an unexpected lump in a part of your body that wasn't there before then it's sensible to act immediately and get it checked out.

That's not being hysterical or irrational – that's a helpful way to think. And anticipating potential problems and having a plan to counteract them is not pessimistic but may actually be considered realistic. Remember, it's a form of loopy logic just to think happy thoughts and believe you'll be immune from problems. It's helpful to weigh up risks and take precautions when necessary. You may remember I've referred to this previously as 'worth it' rather than 'worthless' worry.

Now it's over to you

So once again it's time for some reflection. List some of your concerns and then decide if the reasons for them are historical, hysterical or helpful. Place a tick in the appropriate box recognizing that there could be more than one reason why you're feeling and thinking the way you are. You may revisit some of your issues from the previous exercise or come up with some different ones.

Issue	Historical (based on a past experience)	Hysterical (based on an irrational fear that is unlikely to happen)	Helpful (a realistic and rational assessment of a potential problem or challenge)
1.	☐	☐	☐
2.	☐	☐	☐
3.	☐	☐	☐
4.	☐	☐	☐
5.	☐	☐	☐

This analysis once again helps bring your concern out into the open and helps you clarify if there is a rational reason for your worries, or if you've succumbed to some irrational thinking, fuelled perhaps by an overdeveloped imagination or an unhealthy mental diet consisting of excessive consumption of sensationalized media stories.

Whatever the reason, you are exposing your worries to some form of scrutiny, which in itself can be hugely helpful. By putting them under the spotlight we expose them to any potential flaws (especially if they're based in the hysterical camp), increase our understanding of why we're thinking the way we are (perhaps for historical reasons) and help prepare us to deal with or avoid challenges if our feelings are based upon a helpful understanding of the situation.

The above approach is a particularly strong antidote to the type of loopy logic where we 'wear worry as an identity'.

The real truth is:

> Worry and anxiety are descriptions of your behaviour and how you're feeling rather than descriptions of your character and identity

Now onto our third insight from how to develop a Triple A strategy.

Action

So far we've increased our awareness of what type of stress we're experiencing: situational, anticipatory or residual; and the reasons for our worries: historical, hysterical or helpful. We're now in a place to do something about it.

And it's important that we do. As Dale Carnegie said, 'Our issue is not ignorance but inaction'. Actually, I think it could be a combination of both, but he's definitely got a point. Now in order to explore what actions we can take to deal with our worries we're going to move onto the second great way to use your rational brain. This approach builds upon the Triple A strategy with the emphasis on uncovering the resources we have or need to tackle our worries.

2. Increasing your Influence

In his book *The Seven Habits of Highly Effective People* (Simon & Schuster, 1989), Dr Stephen R. Covey explores the following model in his first habit, 'Be proactive':

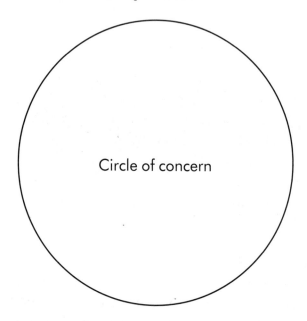

Dr Covey explains that we each have a number of issues in life that can concern us. These could be anything from our health, paying the bills, maintaining relationships, issues related to work, the weather, the future of the economy and the threat of a possible terrorist attack. Whatever these concerns (or worries) might be, they can determine where we focus our time and energy. Some of the issues we place within our circle of concern we'll have little or no control over, but there will be others that we can do something about. Dr Covey states that those things we can influence could be placed within a smaller circle that we call our circle of influence:

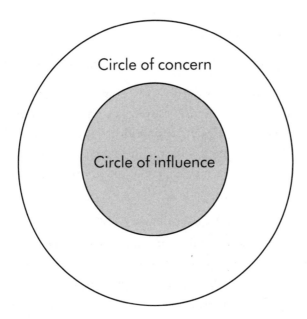

By determining which of these two circles we focus most of our time and energy on we can discover, according to Dr Covey, the degree of our proactivity.

So why don't you press pause for a moment, think about the following categories and decide which ones are within your circle of influence and which aren't.

Here's the list:

- health

- finances

- maintaining your relationships

- work issues

- the weather

- the future of the economy

- threats of terrorist attacks.

So which of these do you have no real significant influence over?

Clearly the weather is outside your control. You can travel to certain places where there is a strong possibility of experiencing the weather you desire (and if your ideal day is grey and raining then you're welcome to visit me in Manchester anytime), but once you're in a place your actions alone won't influence the weather.

Second, unless you happen to be part of a terrorist organization then there's very little you can do to influence whether or not a terrorist attack occurs. Yes you can be vigilant and report anything suspicious, but there's very little you can actually do to prevent a possible attack.

Likewise with the economy and whether or not interest rates go up or down, I think it's fair to say your influence on that probably equates to zero.

Here's the real truth:

People spend vast amounts of time worrying about things over which they have no control

The first three examples were fairly straightforward, but the next ones are less so.

Health comes much more under your influence, but there may be some genetic factors that you have little control over. Some diseases are hereditary, whilst others such as type 2 diabetes are due to lifestyle. So some aspects of your health overlap both circles.

Work issues could be the same. Whether or not your company decides to make people redundant is unlikely to be determined by you. However, how you deal with a colleague, a customer or a particular work challenge will come under your sphere of influence.

The same goes for maintaining relationships and managing your finances, which to a large extent will be influenced by your own actions, but won't be completely in your control.

So thinking about which circle your issue is in is a great starting point, but you'll find the following illustration develops the idea even further. In this instance we're focusing more on a sliding scale of influence as seen below:

0	1	2	3	4	5	6	7	8	9	10

No control	Very little control	A moderate amount of influence	A reasonable amount of influence	A large amount of influence	Total control

This recognizes that our levels of influence can and do vary as opposed to being inside or outside the circle of influence.

The scale of influence

Now, if you combine our scale of influence with how important an issue is to you, you'll gain more insight into the causes of your worries and anxieties.

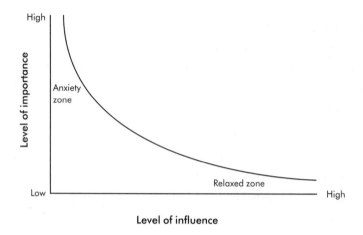

Level of influence

As you'll see, the higher the perceived importance of an issue combined with a low level of influence then the greater chance we'll experience worry, anxiety and stress. Likewise, when our levels of influence are high but the situation is perceived to be of low importance then we are likely to feel relaxed and far less likely to worry.

Now, clearly defining what is and isn't important to us can reduce our anxieties (sometimes we fall into the trap of making trivial stuff important and therefore worry about far more things than we really need to). However, in this section our focus is going to be on developing ways in which we can increase our influence. In doing so we can determine what actions we need to take to improve our situation and therefore decrease our worries.

How influential are you?

What we'll refer to as 'the scale of influence' can be used to determine what level of influence you believe you have in a situation. Now you may have come across a particular prayer which is often referred to as the Serenity Prayer. Whether you pray or not, it does contain an important insight which I want to explore further.

The prayer is most commonly attributed to the American theologian Reinhold Niebuhr (1892–1971). In its most common form it reads as follows:

> *'God, grant me the serenity to accept the things I cannot change,*
> *the courage to change the things I can,*
> *and the wisdom to know the difference.'*

Interestingly the 'prayer' has been adopted by Alcoholics Anonymous and other programmes designed to aid people recover from addiction and compulsion. Personally, I believe it deserves a wider audience and you don't need to be addicted to something in order to benefit from it. The prayer is encouraging us to focus on what we can influence and to recognize there are some things that are beyond our control.

The key point I want to focus on from the prayer is the last line:

> *'and the wisdom to know the difference.'*

Let me elaborate. Imagine you have heard your organization has lost an existing contract and as a result is about to make redundancies. Have a look at the scale of influence on the previous page. Where would you place yourself on the scale given that news?

You see, I think some people would put themselves right at the bottom of the scale in the 'no control' or possibly 'very little control' zone.

But is it possible that someone else, even in the same circumstances, could actually place themselves higher on the scale?

You see, to some extent the amount of influence and control you have could be down to your perception and how you see the situation. And the greater level of influence you believe you have in a situation the more likely you are to take action.

Here's a great example of just that.

Several years ago I was working with an organization that was about to close. I along with several other consultants had been hired to provide support for the staff about to lose their jobs with regard to job search skills, interview techniques and sourcing appropriate training.

We arrived on site in February, three months before the planned closure.

Although staff could not influence the future of the organization, how they responded to the closure was definitely within their sphere of influence. Within the first few weeks of opening what was called 'The Job Shop', we were inundated with people wanting help with CV writing and strategies on how to perform at job interviews.

However, after that initial surge of interest we became aware that over 30% of staff had failed to make contact or seek any help.

Perhaps they didn't need to.

Maybe they already had another job lined up, or were planning to work freelance or start their own business.

But finally, after repeated attempts, we managed to meet some more staff in our final two weeks of the project.

The people I finally got to meet contrasted sharply with those who contacted us when we first arrived. Whereas the initial group could have been defined by their proactiveness and energy, this final group seemed far more passive, and spoke and behaved with a sense of inevitability and resignation regarding their future.

To be fair many of them were aged 45 and over. But their perception of themselves and their future was that their destiny had now been decided. They believed the chances of them working again at their age were slim. They might, they conceded, secure a low-paid job but quite frankly they now felt they were already firmly stuck onto the scrap heap of life. In their mind there was nothing they could do to influence their future. Their birth certificate had seen to that.

Yet there had been people of a similar age who had already been proactive in their job search. Some had actually gained new positions before their own factory was closed permanently, whilst others were already well down the road to starting their own business.

Here's the real truth:

> The difference between some people is not their circumstances but their attitudes

One group perceived they could still influence their future, the other group didn't.

And here's what's interesting.

Sometimes a little self-delusion in tackling a challenge can be helpful.

Remember I said sometimes.

Let me explain.

The Journal of Personality and Social Psychology reports that people who are more accurate and realistic in their assessment of their ability to control the environment seem less mentally healthy and more depressed than those who inaccurately overestimate their sense of control.

So why should those who actually think they have more influence and control over a situation than they actually do be more mentally healthy?

Well, perhaps if you believe you have more influence you are more willing to keep trying to positively affect your environment. You don't give up too easily. You persist. And you might get some breaks that never would have occurred if you'd given up earlier.

Right, let's go back to those people facing redundancy. Their challenge was not just the event, but their attitude towards the event and also themselves. Perhaps some never sought help because they were lost in the loopy logic and 'just thinking happy thoughts'.

'Something will turn up. It's bound to.'

Maybe they believed luck would be on their side and they would simply find themselves in the right place at the right time.

But this approach is not increasing your influence; it's leaving things to fate.

And that can be fatal.

Perhaps other people failed to seek help because they were lost in another type of loopy logic – 'Playing the victim'. They see their future as completely in the hands of others – and believe their age has determined a less than bright future.

And do you know what?

These beliefs usually tend to be proven right. They really do. People push fewer doors – if indeed any – and then wonder why a door hasn't opened for them yet. They have inadvertently created a self-fulfilling prophecy, and in doing so demonstrate a lack of wisdom in knowing what they can and cannot change.

OK, enough about other people.

Now it's over to you

This is now where things can begin to change for you. You're no longer looking at examples of other people's situations – it's time to focus on you. It's time to see how by engaging your rational brain you can identify what influence you have over a situation, and what you can and cannot control.

Excited?

Hope so.

Here goes.

Identify two situations that currently concern you. (Although similar to our previous exercises, we're now focusing more on actually resolving them, not just being aware or analyzing our worries.) The language you use to describe how you feel about these situations may vary from 'worried', 'anxious', 'stressed' or some other alternatives, but whatever the description it's very much an issue for you.

To do this exercise you might want to find a pen and paper, or whatever other form of technology you use to record your thoughts. My preference is slate and a piece of chalk, but that's probably my northern background coming through.

First write down your issue or concern. Please do this. The temptation is to just think about it, but actually there is tremendous benefit in getting your thoughts down onto paper/screen/slate. For a start it helps create clarity. It forces you to articulate clearly what your actual issues are. Sometimes people have muddled or muddy thinking. They know they have a concern which results in a lack of peace or wellbeing, but they've not actually pinned down what the actual issue is. Recording your thoughts is a great way to do this.

My friend Richard talks about 'fuzzy worry', whereby he has a lot of generalized issues and concerns spinning round in his mind. The antidote for him is to offload his worries onto a whiteboard so that the fuzziness gives way to clarity.

The following 'triggers' should help stimulate and clear your thinking. Work through them for each issue you've identified.

- My real issue is ...

- In terms of importance, on a scale of 1–10 (where 10 = death) my issue is probably a _____ (write down the number).

- My concern about this situation is ...

- The impact this is having on me is ...

LET'S GET RATIONAL / **141**

- As a result I find myself doing …

- As a result I find myself not doing …

- The best way to describe how I feel about this is …

- As a result the behaviour you would notice from me is …

- As a result the impact it has on others around me is …

- When I consider the issue and think about my level of influence (see scale on p. 133) it probably is around …

- The actions I have taken so far to help myself with this issue are …

- When I reflect on what else I can do to influence the situation I realize I could also …

- The limits (if any) I have in influencing this situation are …

- The people I could talk to and who may be able to help me in some way would be …

- If there was one single action I could take to improve my situation it would be to …

- Realistically I could start implementing this single action …

OK, now let me be honest with you – I have a concern, which is this:

You've not done the above exercise.

You've simply skimmed through the statements.

Bad move.

You can't rush on to the next section hoping to find the magic bullet to your problems. You have to be prepared not just simply to read this book but also to engage with it. That means taking some time out for you to do the exercise. Clearly if you don't that's of no real concern to me, but actually I know you would benefit from doing so and find this book of greater value than if you didn't.

Now I'm not here to pry into your life, but here's a challenge for you. Since you've started reading this book we have to some extent entered a form of relationship. I've aimed not simply to impart information but also some insight into my own personal world. I'm a great believer in keeping this material real and sharing from real world experience.

Now I want to give you the opportunity to do the same.

I would love to hear about your reflections from the above exercise. I'm not expecting you to send me your answers to all the trigger statements (although if it helps I'll be absolutely fine with that). But it would be great to receive your insights. I promise I will read your email and send you a reply.

By doing so I'm not wanting to set myself up as an advisor or therapist, but as someone who you can connect with. For whatever reason you might not want to share your reflections with someone close to you (although I hope you can), but by sending your thoughts to someone who doesn't know you and who is not emotionally involved in your world, it could give you the gentle push you need to actually do the exercise.

My email address is Paul.McGee@theSUMOguy.com and anything you send will be confidential. Promise.

Finally, as a way of helping you see things in perspective and reminding yourself to focus on what actions you can take to improve your situation, commit to memory the following two questions. Trust me, you'll find them of huge benefit:

- **Where is this issue on a scale of 1–10 (where 10 = death)?**

- **How can I influence or improve this situation?**

And for your own personal mantra, how about you adopt this one:

> I focus on what I can influence and let go of the rest

Hammock time

Well, you've had an opportunity to do a lot of reflecting in this section on a couple of issues so my only other questions to you are these.

- What would be your main insights and reflections from doing the above exercise?
- As a result of doing the exercise, has where you see your level of control on the scale of influence changed at all?
- When you read earlier in the chapter about the closure of the factory, which response from staff did you most identify with?

In a nutshell

- Rational brain is on hand and at your service. You simply need to know how to best utilize its services.
- Develop a Triple A strategy firstly through Awareness. Reflect on whether your stress is situational, anticipatory or residual.
- Analyze your worry by determining whether the causes of it are historical, hysterical or helpful. Deal with the root, not just the fruit.
- Action is the ultimate key to tackling your worry habit, and this becomes far easier to do when you've increased your awareness and analyzed the causes.
- Look at ways of increasing your sphere of influence. Some things are out of your control. Period. But there are still many things you can do to influence most situations.
- Overestimating your ability to influence and control a situation can be positive as long as it's not overdone.
- Writing about your worries can bring a sense of clarity and perspective. It helps reduce fuzzy worry.

Chapter 6

Manage Your Imagination

I was tempted to call this chapter 'Use Your Imagination,' but there was no need. You see, you're using your imagination all the time. From the moment you wake and think about what you've planned that day to just before you crash out to sleep and reflect on what you've done, you're using your imagination.

We use it even in seemingly mundane situations. Can't remember where you parked your car? You use your imagination to help you remember where you parked it. What are you going to have for dinner tonight? You use your imagination to help you picture it and the ingredients you will need. But interestingly although we're using it all the time we often do so without even realizing it. And here's the real truth:

How you use your imagination can seriously affect your anxiety levels

Let's see why.

Napoleon Bonaparte said 'Most people's lives are the result of mismanaged imagination.'

I think he had a point.

You see, you and I are movie directors. Maybe not quite on the scale of Spielberg or Tarantino, but we make them all the same.

Let me explain. You're about to use your imagination to help you remember a list of ten items.

Now just humour me for a moment and play along. I promise it will be worth the effort.

Imagine a large **drill** drilling into a large bar of green soap. Out of the **soap** I want you to imagine green **paint** shooting up into the air. Notice that as the paint falls, some of it falls onto a large metal **padlock**. Visualize the padlock covered in green paint. Notice that it's attached to the door of a **caravan**. See the caravan in your mind's eye. See it swaying from side to side. Why? I want you to imagine its being pulled down a motorway by a purple **Rolls Royce**. Now imagine who's driving the Rolls Royce – it's **David Beckham**. As you visualize him you see that on his head he's wearing a black and yellow **top hat**, in his mouth he has two pieces of **chocolate** protruding out like two chicken legs and he's wearing a pair of green and white spotted football **shorts**.

OK, now review the list for a second time and then close your eyes and imagine those pictures being replayed over in your mind. Go on then. Don't start reading ahead because you can't be bothered. Have a go at doing it now. You'll benefit much more from this chapter if you do.

Now my guess is that if you can take a little time you would actually be able to remember all ten items that I've given you.

And how did you do that?

Simply by using your imagination. I gave you some very specific words and immediately, through the power of your imagination, you created images in your mind in order to visualize those words.

Now, without trying to big up the exercise too much, you and I created a short mental movie in your mind. I gave you the script, you developed the movie. And to be honest it's not that hard to do. Agree?

OK, now let me give you something else to visualize in your head – 'Breakfast.'

Now as you pictured that in your mind did you visualize the word 'breakfast' written in black on a white background or did you imagine a bowl of cereal, fruit and yoghurt or perhaps a plate of sausages, eggs and bacon?

My guess is it was the latter. You created pictures and images in your mind and not words. You see, that's how most of us are wired to think. Not so much in words but in images.

Now here's what's interesting.

We do exactly the same when we worry about a forthcoming event. We create a short mental movie in our mind and this time you're the one with the script.

Let's take this further. Ever heard of the phrase 'things went pear shaped', i.e. they went wrong? Well let's use that word 'pear' as an acronym to illustrate the link between our imagination, the pictures we have inside our head and its impact on how we feel and behave.

Imagine that a particular task you hate to do is giving a presentation in front of a group of colleagues and important customers.

Let's also imagine that a future promotion is riding on the impact you make during this presentation.

Now, imagine that you absolutely hate and detest presentations. (Which for many people won't be that hard to do!) OK, let's work through P.E.A.R:

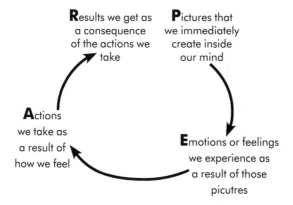

Right, now let's relate the P.E.A.R. process to making that presentation. Imagine the first picture that you created in your head, or popped into your mind, was a group of unhappy customers and colleagues listening to your presentation. Or you imagined your mouth feeling dry and you forgetting your words. Or the PowerPoint not working. Or you spilling your coffee over your boss as you stood up to speak. Let your mind wander at this stage as you conjure up a range of negative scenarios.

Notice how you're feeling. Without having to give it too much thought you are already creating a short story inside your head. To be fair, it might only be the seeds of a story, but you've got the capability to turn it into an entire trilogy. Would it be fair to say that imagining a series of negative events would influence your emotions and how you're feeling? Would an accurate description of how you might feel be anxiety, or possibly even panic? Could that anxiety influence what actions you decide to now take? Could those actions potentially include asking to be pulled out of the presentation, to feign an illness, or even to phone a colleague and ask them to stand in for you?

Now, of course those fearful feelings could actually be the motivator you need to prepare well, seek support and get some practice in, but whatever actions we take the reality is it all starts with our imagination.

You see, you decide whether those mental images you focus on derail you or drive you. Derail you from success or drive you to achieving it. The real truth is:

> You can direct the movies in your mind

And guess what? At any stage of the process you have the ability to shout 'Cut!'

In fact you can decide to play the whole scene again but create a different outcome. You're in charge. It might not always seem that way, but after that initial thought or image has popped up in your head you can then decide the rest of the story. How about you try that some time? When you find yourself imagining fearful thoughts, just say to yourself 'Cut'. Hey, if you're on your own at the time you might even want to say it out loud. Clearly doing so whilst on a crowded train, plane or tube may not be too appropriate, and if you're a surgeon performing an operation that might not be a good time to use that phrase. But trust me, joking aside, it can work.

Alternatively you could say 'Continue.' Allow the movie in your mind to continue after you've had your fearful thoughts fuelled by the question 'What if?', but then follow it with the question 'What then?' It's in your control to imagine dealing successfully with your situation, even when you allow yourself to imagine things going wrong. You can still get to come up with a better ending.

Why is our imagination important?

Well we've got our evolutionary make-up to thank for our imagination. As Todd Buchholz writes, 'Our ability to imagine the future is an extraordinary evolutionary gift.'

Albert Einstein agreed, stating 'Imagination is more important than knowledge.' It's what makes us different from the rest of the animal kingdom. Our ability to imagine means we're able to forward-wind to the future. That's exciting. It helps us to plan and prepare. It's what causes us to feel excitement as we plan a holiday or a special occasion.

It's what can also help us anticipate potential problems and challenges. This ability has made us the most successful animal on planet Earth.

All good.

So far.

But there's also a price to pay. Your imagination can be both a blessing and a curse. You see, as a species, thinking about the future also allows us to realize that we are both mortal and vulnerable.

If left unchecked, our imagination can imprison us in false fear. Don't just take my word for it. Read what Dr Andrew Weil of the University of Arizona Medical School has to say:

> *If you don't use your imagination skilfully it can be hijacked by your fears. Reclaiming control of your imagination can let you use*

its creativity, wisdom and motivational power to solve problems and enjoy life more.' (Taken from the foreword of the book *The Worry Solution*, Dr Martin Rossman, Rider Books, 2010)

See, I told you it was important.

Why fuss over fear?

We've explored earlier how fear can be a gift. But if we're not careful fear can also rob us of enjoying life.

An acronym for the word fear that you may be familiar with is:

False

Evidence

Appearing

Real

Well another similar definition would be:

Future

Events

Appearing

Real

Of course it's entirely down to how you use your imagination as to whether this future event fits into the psychological suspense/horror category, or something a little lighter. After all, you're the movie director remember. But when it comes to facing life's challenges many of us fail to adopt the light romantic comedy approach to future events. That's not necessarily a bad thing.

Fear used wisely can help us foresee potential problems and prepare ourselves to do something about them. The problem is, fear isn't always channelled wisely.

You may recall from our previous chapter that worry is also known as 'anticipatory stress'. In other words our imagination can trigger the stress response over an event that has yet to occur. And so creative are some people that these future events have cataclysmic consequences that their imagination convinces them are real. The real truth is:

> As humans we're the only animals that create stress with our own minds

This, coupled with a large dose of loopy logic, can persuade people that, as it's been so easy to imagine a particular outcome, then there is a real risk that it will occur. As a result of your unmanaged imagination, your anxiety increases and your body prepares itself for fight or flight over something that hasn't even happened.

Amazing, eh? That's how powerful and influential your imagination can be. It can be used to create something as beautiful and outstanding as the Taj Mahal, and yet this very same piece of brain software can create a group of frightened and fearful creatures – namely us. It can be the author of a sense of calm or panic. It can trigger ideas and inspiration. It literally knows no limits.

But allowing your imagination unbridled freedom when fuelled by fear can severely limit your sense of peace and enjoyment of life. Like an unbroken wild horse, we need to learn how to bring it under control and harness its ability to work for and not against us.

And that's precisely what we're going to do now.

Ready?

Using your imagination to work for you

My close friends have a gorgeous daughter called Anna. For several years Anna has had an imaginary friend called Robert. Robert has been a playmate, particularly at home, and it would seem also a scapegoat when things have broken or been damaged. It seems quite convenient having this imaginary friend, who needs no feeding, is happy to do whatever you do and seems quite happy to take the rap for things you've done wrong. It's certainly worked for Anna. She's 42.

Just kidding.

She's now seven and if I'm honest I'm not sure how big a part Robert plays in her life anymore. But it got me thinking.

I'm significantly older than Anna but I too have imaginary friends. In fact one of them died years ago and I've yet to meet several of them.

Let me explain.

One of my imaginary friends is Ernest Shackleton. He was an Anglo-Irish Antarctic explorer who is probably best known for leading the 'Endurance' mission after the First World War. After his ship sank he spent his time along with his crew living on floating ice before eventually making an amazing trip lasting 16 days in a small boat to South Georgia, where they were eventually rescued.

Now I've been hugely impressed and inspired by Shackleton's resourcefulness, courage and determination. I have yet to lead a team of men to the South Pole, although taking my children shopping on a Saturday when they were younger did seem equally challenging. However, I do have some rather hectic and demanding travel schedules at times and I often find myself asking 'How would Shackleton handle this?' or 'What would Shackleton say about this situation?' In a sense I hold an imaginary conversation with a man who died nearly 90 years ago. But that's the power of your imagination.

Now I realize this may sound bizarre, but it's true. And perhaps more importantly it helps me.

Taking this idea a little further, I was coaching a woman, Shelley, who had real confidence issues about presenting to groups of people.

I asked her to think of a female role model, living or dead, whom she admired.

She chose Madonna the singer (as opposed to the iconic religious figure).

I then asked her to imagine what thoughts Madonna would have about making a presentation. What would her attitude and approach be? If she felt nervous would she show it? I elaborated further and discussed with Shelley whether she had ever been upset about something but put on a brave face and acted as if everything was fine.

She had.

'Good. In that case you've proved you do have some acting skills.'

Now I wanted Shelley to act as if she was adopting the positive attributes of Madonna's character.

To actually take on some of her persona.

Will it feel strange?

Of course it will.

But just as an actor can take on a role and literally become someone else, Shelley could do something similar.

I wasn't asking her to perform as if she was at a concert, and it was perfectly acceptable to wear her own clothes and not prance into a presentation wearing a conical bra and fishnet tights; but I wanted her to be and think with a more Madonna-type attitude.

Her focus changed from what she didn't want to be – shy, nervous and hesitant in front of a group – and to focus more on how she did want to behave. Using her imagination to Madonna-ize herself somewhat really seemed to help. And apart from beginning her presentation with the line 'Like a virgin, touched for the very first time' it actually seemed to work rather well for her.

OK, I know what you're wondering. This seems a little bit weird, perhaps even bordering on wacky.

Well, I understand where you're coming from, but how many people use their imagination to crush their confidence by creating images in their minds that immediately trigger feelings of anxiety and dread.

Now that's what I call wacky.

If Shelley finds acting a little like Madonna helps her to behave with more confidence, why shouldn't she adopt this technique?

And if I find having an imaginary conversation with a deceased explorer (I'm not suggesting I'm actually speaking to a dead person, in case you were wondering) helps me tackle some challenges with a degree more positivity, then why shouldn't I?

I'm a pragmatist.

My underlying question with any of this stuff is 'Will it work?' 'Is it practical?' You see, there are some further wonderful ways to use your imagination to calm yourself down. But they often involve you finding a place of peace and tranquillity, preferably whilst wearing loose clothing, where you've got at least half an hour to do the exercise of relaxing your body and allowing your imagination to take you to a special place.

This is great.

If you have the time.

And the discipline.

And if it fits with your personality.

But if I'm honest, whilst recognizing its benefits, it doesn't really fit with either my lifestyle or personality. And if it does fit with yours you're probably doing this already.

So I tend to use imagination exercises that I can literally do any time, any place, anywhere. I've even been stuck in a traffic jam late for an appointment and found myself imagining a large watering can pouring droplets of peace onto my head.

Does it work all the time?

158 / HOW NOT TO WORRY

No.

Does it instantly eliminate all my anxiety?

No.

So why do it?

Well, whilst I'm using my imagination in this way it's not allowing any air time to use my imagination in a way that could well escalate my anxiety.

And although I admit it doesn't eliminate my anxiety completely, it does reduce and control it.

You don't think I'd really carry on doing it if it didn't, do you?

I'm not that weird.

Really, I'm not.

Despite what my kids will tell you.

More ways to use your imagination

Recently I had what I considered some unfair criticism from some members of a group I was working with. The majority had appreciated both my style and content, but two people took particular exception to the fact that I mentioned that I'd worked with a premiership football team. They perceived that as 'bigging myself up' unnecessarily.

Perhaps they had a point.

If I'm honest, I do enjoy my work with this particular team.

And I'm aware that there are thousands of people who would love to be in my position.

But my critics said I made constant reference to this fact.

I know I didn't.

I also know that along with my occasional success I also talk about my struggles both past and present.

I'm happy to admit that I lost my job through ill health, and only started my own business because I was unable to get a job as I couldn't pass a medical. And I talk about the mistakes I've made whilst growing my business.

Why am I telling you this? Because, if I'm honest, their criticism nagged at me.

I briefly imagined what they said after I had left the session.

The movie began to play in my mind.

And then I realized what I was doing.

'Cut.'

I needed to stop this internal movie – and as I was the producer and director I had the power to do so.

I then changed scenes in my mind. I thought about my mate Charles, who despite his posh name is a fellow Mancunian now living in Toronto. I imagined having a conversation with him about the comments.

What would he say?

How would he respond?

My mood began to change.

I began to smile.

Yes, I needed to be careful and perhaps sensitive around people regarding some of my work and how I talked about it, but imagining a conversation with Charles put things into perspective.

I calmed down.

I moved on.

And the funny thing is, Charles in reality hasn't got a flipping clue about the incident or how his 'advice' helped me!

That's the power of your imagination.

Problem solving with a little help from your friends

Clearly a major cause of worry and anxiety can come from problems we face but which we're unsure of how best to approach. Perhaps our first port of call would be to approach friends and family for their perspective.

Fine.

If they can give you some sound advice.

But how can I put this nicely?

What if to a large extent they're as clueless as you are?

Apologies.

That wasn't very nice.

But do you get my point?

OK, well here's another way in which your imagination could come in rather handy.

Write a list of people you respect, either living or dead, who have some expertise in the area you're currently struggling with.

They don't have to be famous.

They just need to be people you have some degree of respect for.

You don't even have to like them.

Let's assume, as an example, that you've got a career or business decision you have to make. Who could be some of the people who in an ideal world you would like to ask for their advice?

Richard Branson? Well certainly he might be appropriate, although I think I'd seek fashion advice from someone else.

Lord Alan Sugar?

Duncan Bannatyne?

Karren Brady?

Michelle Mone?

Walt Disney?

Steve Jobs?

Jim Collins?

Stephen Fry?

Stephen Hawking?

I'm just listing a few names that come to me. You might not recognize them all.

Fine.

Paul Sandham would be another.

It's unlikely you've heard of him.

He's a mate.

He's been a mentor and friend to me. So too is Richard Farrow. Like I say, they don't need to be famous.

Now, rather than seek advice from just one of them, perhaps hold a board meeting (in your mind) and invite all of them.

Again, I know this may sound a little crazy, but why don't you pose the problem to your board of directors? (Remember though, you have the final say.) Imagine from what knowledge you have of them, what questions they might have and what ideas they may come up with.

Trust your intuition on this.

You could have some real fun with this.

You could even play this imaginary game with a few friends. You each take it in turn to play the role of a different person.

Hey, do the accents if you want.

Imagine chairing the meeting.

'Er … just a moment, Lord Sugar, I don't think Richard has finished his point yet.'

You could write down some thoughts that might come from your imaginary board of directors.

Now you really think I'm crazy don't you?

Why?

How many positive ideas and insights do you have locked up within you that, by using your imagination, you might actually unlock?

And if you are stressing over a decision and feel you haven't got anyone to turn to, then what have you got to lose by doing this kind of exercise?

This experience may be a complete waste of time.

There again … it might not.

But you'll never know.

Unless you try it.

So next time you ring my office and hear I'm in a meeting, it could be with literally anyone.

'Sorry, he's just tied up with Abraham Lincoln at the moment, can I get him you call you later?'

The great thing about your imagination is that it gives you the luxury of being able to bring in a new group of special advisors to consult with over different matters. Who you choose is dependent on your situation.

Now it's over to you

Right, it's that time again. Time to put the ball in your court. Now as I've pointed out earlier, most people who are asked to do an exercise in a book usually skim over it completely and go to the next page.

What about you?

Will you be like *most* people?

Or will you actually do the exercise?

Go on.

Be different.

At the very least do this in your head and ideally write your answers down if not in the book in a place that you can access easily.

Now give this some thought.

Below are five categories.

You have to come up with *up to* four advisors for each category whom you could imagine seeking advice from. Remember they don't necessarily need to be living or famous. Who would be the people you would like to consult for advice if there were no limits on whom you could choose?

Career/work

1.   3.

2.   4.

Health/wellbeing

1.   3.

2.   4.

Relationships (personal)

1.   3.

2.   4.

Relationships (professional)

1.   3.

2.   4.

General life advice/wisdom

1.   3.

2.   4.

Now when you're faced with a particular challenge and you find yourself worrying, why not seek out some help from your imaginary friends. However, don't go too far with this. I'm not suggesting if things go wrong you start to blame them.

'This is all the Dalai Lama's fault.'

No. That was a strategy Anna used, when she blamed her friend Robert. But to be fair to her she hadn't started school when she did so.

Take responsibility for the choices you make, but use your amazing imagination to help you explore and uncover more of those choices and reduce more of your worries.

Hammock time

- So how much do you allow your imagination to trigger worry and anxiety in yourself?
- Has this anxiety just affected you or have there been times when you've spread your anxiety amongst others?
- What have been your thoughts on having imaginary conversations with people both living and dead?
- How comfortable have you felt doing the exercises?
- What have been your two main insights from this chapter?

In a nutshell

- We're using our imagination constantly – often without realizing it.
- Imagination can be a powerful positive force. It can also trigger high levels of anxiety. It all depends on where you allow your imagination to take you.
- Pictures in our mind lead to Emotions, which can influence our Actions which will in turn lead to Results. (P.E.A.R.)
- Worrying about the future requires you to use your imagination, which is often referred to as anticipatory stress.
- Perhaps imaginary friends are not just for children, although who yours are may remain a closely guarded secret.
- By using your imagination in a creative and fun way you can unlock ideas and insights that you would not normally have accessed, which can help tackle your worries.

Chapter 7

Show a Little Respect...
to Yourself

Imagine you owned a thoroughbred racehorse. You've invested a considerable amount of money in order to own it.

So would you exercise it?

Would you ensure it had a proper diet?

Would you give it the care and attention it needs?

Would you call for the vet if there seemed to be a health issue?

Would you hire the support of others to ensure it thrived and reached its potential?

I've got a sneaky feeling you would do all of the above, wouldn't you?

In fact you'd be mad not to.

Agree?

OK, so what's my point?

Well, I'm guessing you may not be responsible for the upkeep of a thoroughbred horse.

But you are responsible for something even more valuable.

Yourself.

But do you look after yourself as you would this horse?

Take enough exercise?

Have a balanced diet?

Have regular health checks?

Hire the support of others?

Do what you can to reach your potential?

Well, whatever your answers to the above, that's what this chapter is about. Perhaps by showing a little more respect to yourself you'll actually avoid feeling stressed and worried, and when such a scenario is unrealistic you'll still be in a better place to deal with your pressures more effectively.

So let's explore five ways we can show ourselves respect.

1. Start changing your scripts

The reality is that when it comes to the whole issue surrounding worry, stress and anxiety, we can be the author of our own downfall. Compared to that thoroughbred horse, we can actually treat ourselves with far less care and compassion. You see, whereas we would often feel angry and upset if someone continually spoke to us in a negative way, we seem quite willing to allow such a verbal assault when we're the originator. But here's the real truth:

> Dealing effectively with the challenges of life means recognizing that what we think about ourselves is vitally important

Our internal conversations are significant.

A top sportsperson wouldn't start saying to themselves at the beginning of a competition:

'I'm so awful, there's no way I'm going to win today.'

'I feel so lethargic and unfit; I don't know why I've even bothered turning up.'

Not if they want to perform at their best they wouldn't

OK, I admit they may occasionally find themselves slipping into this kind of thinking, but they know they cannot afford to stay there.

Such negative and disempowering thoughts may arrive as an unexpected guest in our minds but you don't actually have to spend the rest of the day entertaining them.

Agree?

Now this next bit is crucial to understand.

When you find yourself at the wrong end of such conversations, you need to realize you can control how long and how intense that internal chatter lasts. Just as we explored in Chapter 6, 'Manage Your Imagination', you can be the movie director of what's going on inside your head. And if your imagination is creating the pictures you see on the screen, remember you're also responsible for the accompanying script.

So be really careful what you say to yourself, because your inner thoughts can be a self-defeating form of self-suggestion. And these suggestions can distort and amplify your anxieties and worries to a far higher level than they need to be. You can literally increase your emotional intensity by what you say to yourself.

So be careful of thinking or saying the following:

'I just don't know how I'm ever going to cope. I'm at my wits end.'

'Everything is getting me down at the moment and I can't see it ever ending.'

'Just when I think I'm getting on top of things, something else comes along and takes me back to square one.'

'I'm convinced someone up there doesn't like me.'

'This has to be the worst thing that's ever happened to me.'

'Well, as far as I'm concerned it ruined the whole holiday. Everything was bad from start to finish.'

Now clearly some of the above comments could be seen as a cry for help from someone who is indeed struggling in life. And as we've seen previously, when you're emotionally involved in a situation it's difficult to gain a rational perspective on what's actually happening and how we're feeling. In this state what may only be a temporary experience can feel like a permanent outcome.

Most of the time it isn't.

But we need to be aware of the impact these subtle yet self-defeating thought patterns can have.

We can talk ourselves into defeat.

We can talk ourselves into a place of no hope.

We can talk ourselves into an anxious state.

If we're not careful we can magnify our problems and amplify our worries to a deafening crescendo. We can blind ourselves to possibilities. We can convince ourselves there's no way back.

Ultimately our internal thoughts can rob us of a more enjoyable and fulfilling life.

And we can do all the above without even thinking about it.

Amazing, eh?

And do you know the ironic thing about it all?

It's actually our destructive way of thinking that is often at the root of the problem.

You see, we wrongly convince ourselves that it's simply and solely down to our circumstances why we're feeling the way we are. Clearly our circumstances play a huge part, but here's the real truth:

> How we think about our circumstances and our ability to deal with them is crucial to how we're feeling

And although you might not be a professional athlete about to compete at the top level, your thoughts do count.

Big time.

And you're the chief script writer. Life may chip in with an unexpected scene change. Other people may influence how part of the script develops, but ultimately you're in charge.

You're the director, remember.

You're the editor.

You get to decide which dialogue remains in the final cut and which ends up in the bin.

And let's be honest, we cannot guarantee a happy ending.

Life isn't like that.

And some parts of the script cannot be influenced by us.

I said 'some parts.'

Not the entire script.

Remember,

it's not about fate

or luck

or destiny.

It's about you.

Your choices.

Your decisions.

What you decide to include in the script.

And what gets deleted.

It won't always be a happy ending, but with your input it can still be a happier one.

Here are a few lines you might want to include in your revised and updated script, particularly in challenging times:

'*I did the best I could at the time. I've learnt. I'm wiser. I'm moving on.*'

'*With the help of others I know I'll pull through this.*'

'*Everything is temporary, including how I feel.*'

'*This will end. I'll come through the other side.*'

'*Stuff happens. Life doesn't have a vendetta against me.*'

'*I'm thankful and grateful for the many positive things in my life right now.*'

'*It's been a challenge but it's not the end of the world.*'

'*I'm wiser as a result of this experience.*'

'*I can become bitter or better. I'm choosing the latter.*'

'*I'm aware I need support, and I'll make sure I get it.*'

'*I had a worry moment, but I'm OK now.*'

Hammock time

- To what extent can you identify with some negative scripts going on inside your head?
- How long do you tend to entertain them for?
- If you had to choose two statements to say to yourself in challenging times which would they be?

Here's another way in which we show a lack of respect to ourselves and what to do about it.

2. Avoid going it alone

Ancient writings indicate that pride goes before a fall. And it is true that pride can be the cause of the fall. Particularly when pride prevents us from opening up to others. From seeking help. From seeking support.

And it seems to be a prominent trait, especially amongst the male species. Not exclusively their domain, but one they seem to inhabit in greater numbers than their female counterparts.

Maybe it's related to the Alpha Male syndrome. The need for dominance. Power. Control. To be seen in a particular light by others.

Sod that.

Maybe it's a weakness in the eyes of some, but I'm fairly open and honest about my vulnerabilities with people.

I'm also fairly aware of my strengths.

And my limitations.

And I have many.

On a practical level DIY is not my scene.

It holds no real interest for me.

I think I've been wired differently to other people in this regard. I'm convinced that some people's brains go into overdrive when presented by a practical challenge. Their brain circuitry illuminates. Their juices flow. They lick their lips with eager and earnest anticipation, like Pavlov's dog hearing the sound of a bell and expecting to be fed.

But when I'm presented with a practical challenge you actually have to check for signs of life, especially when it's related to erecting flat-packed furniture.

My mouth is dry.

A part of my brain will at that point drift off into a semi-comatose state. The lights may be on but there's no one at home. The wheel's turning but the hamster's dead.

You get my point. If I'm not on my guard I could allow this area of my life to become a source of worry, anxiety and stress if I'm not careful.

So I get help in this area. And to be honest I'm not too proud about where I seek that help from.

My 81 year old mother-in-law is one person who provides some practical support. (Although to be fair the re-roofing of our current house fell a little below my expectations.) My wife Helen also possesses more DIY sense and competence than myself. In some ways she's the magician and I'm her not-so-glamorous assistant.

The point is, I recognize this fact.

My ego can cope.

And although my lack of competence and desire to do DIY is a source of amusement and banter at times, people don't point at me in the street and mock me. Well, not that I've noticed. I don't walk around with a board draped around me with the words 'DIY failure' emblazoned across it.

My children still talk to me.

Sometimes.

My family has not disowned me.

Yet.

I'm comfortable not going alone. I've parked my pride.

And there's many areas in life that are perhaps more significant and important than DIY skills where we need to do exactly the same.

But some people would rather go it alone.

Hide their worries.

Bury their anxieties.

Suppress their stress.

Denial becomes their main defence.

The problem is that's really hard to do.

It's difficult to sustain for a long period.

Meanwhile the issue and its causes remains unresolved.

The real truth is this:

> Depriving yourself of support is like depriving yourself of oxygen

You need it to survive.

Particularly when faced with a big challenge.

And I'm not talking about erecting flat-packed furniture.

I'm being serious.

You may be denying yourself the opportunity of living a more enjoyable life.

Your pride could be preventing you from doing so.

You're more bothered about how others perceive you and of maintaining a certain persona than you are about getting the help you need.

And if that's the case it's important you recognize this.

Parking your pride and seeking support can still be done in a private and low-key way.

We're not talking about a Tiger Woods-type public confession. You don't have to take out a full page advert in your local paper.

But you do have to admit to some people that you need some help.

That person may be a doctor.

Your partner.

A mate.

A counsellor.

Your bank.

Your boss.

A colleague.

A neighbour.

A minister.

A debt counsellor.

The key is you take some action and talk it through with someone, or perhaps get some help.

Now clearly you're not going to go from one extreme to another and start seeking advice from the postman or the sales assistant at the local supermarket. And when people casually ask you 'How are you?' it's not an open invitation to pour out your worries – tempting though that may be.

Ultimately you're not seeking support from a lot of people but you may be seeking a lot of support from some people.

In fact, 'some' may be as few as one or two.

That's OK.

As long as you're not going it alone, deluded by your own misguided belief that you're some superhero capable of dealing with life's challenges singlehanded.

You're not.

And neither are you weak or inadequate for needing the help and support of others.

You're normal.

So step out of that vehicle marked 'pride'. Park it next to the one marked 'denial'. Put away the keys. Decide who and where you need to get some support from. And remember, seeking support could be one of the most important ways in which you show some respect for yourself.

Hammock time

- How comfortable are you seeking support and advice from others?
- If you struggle to do so what would be the main reasons for this?
- Identify some people whom you could seek support from.
- Why these people in particular?
- Now identify an organization that you would approach if necessary.
- In what way do you think they could help you?
- So do you need to contact them? If so, when are you going to do it?

3. Let go of grudges

We talked earlier about residual stress. In other words the event or issue is over but we fail to move on. We re-live. We re-tell. Or perhaps we do the opposite. We store away our pain. We hide our hurts. In this section I want to focus on the self-harm we un-intentionally inflict upon ourselves by failing to allow ourselves to move on.

Earlier in this chapter I highlighted more positive scripts we could use in challenging situations. One phrase was 'I can become bitter or better. I'm choosing the latter.'

The challenge is, do we? Or do we hold onto our bitterness that robs us of getting better?

As Norman Vincent-Peal, author of the self-help classic *The Power of Positive Thinking* (Cedar Books, new edition, 1990), said:

> *'Resentment or grudges do no harm to the person against whom you hold these feelings. They simply eat away at you.'*

Eat away at us? Harm us? Maybe we deceive ourselves into thinking that because we respect ourselves we have a right to hold onto our grudges. Perhaps by letting go and moving on we feel we're letting the other person off lightly. We're trivializing the issue.

That's understandable.

A friend of mine saw his wife leave him for his best friend.

He was betrayed by the people closest to him.

People he trusted.

My friend was devastated.

Angry.

Bitter.

A necessary part of the emotional rollercoaster that he must inevitably go on.

What happened has the potential to ruin his life.

But harsh as this may sound, whether it does or not is not down to his ex-wife or best friend.

It's down to him.

He can feed his bitterness.

Nurture it.

Keep it fresh and alive.

Or over time allow it to be starved of what it needs to survive.

It won't die off straight away.

Like some desert plants it can be highly resilient.

And my suggestion is not for him to passively accept what has happened or to quickly forgive, forget and move on.

He's not a machine.

But he can decide what he chooses to focus on.

What he chooses to think and talk about.

Or he can gradually destroy himself.

You see, bitterness strangles our sense of peace and wellbeing. It sucks the energy out of a fulfilling life.

Now the scar will probably never go. But let me tell you this.

It will fade over time.

But if you continue to pick at the scabs the wound will never heal. By re-telling and re-living you're reinforcing the pain.

Here's the real truth:

You can't start the next chapter of your life if you keep re-reading the last one

For my friend, healing will take a long time in this case.

You can't rush recovery.

But you can do a great deal to lengthen the process.

And sometimes you can prevent recovery from ever happening.

Seek justice by all means, but recognize that revenge is a powerful way of harming yourself. What you think is a way of preserving your self-respect is actually damaging it.

And let's get some perspective here. I chose to focus on a serious issue in this example. But people can allow their bitterness plant to blossom over far more insignificant things.

A parking space being 'stolen.'

A driver cutting you up.

Someone forgetting your birthday.

A friend ignoring you.

A boss not giving you the credit you deserve.

A stranger being rude.

As I wrote in a previous book, 'Don't waste your emotional energy getting angry with strangers you'll never meet again. Pity them or laugh at them. But save your anger for something more worthwhile.'

You see, holding onto grudges nourishes the soil in which bitterness grows.

It's time to stop feeding it.

(It's important to note that there may be cases when due to the trauma and severity of the event you need some form of professional help. A good starting place would be to visit your doctor.)

Hammock time

- Is there an incident from your past that you now need to call time on, i.e. it's something you no longer need to talk about?
- You might find it helpful to write down what this issue is and then either burn it or bin it. This symbolic act can be a way of helping you let go.

As you will have noticed, I've kept this Hammock time deliberately short. In this case it's not constructive to reflect too much on your issue. You've probably already done enough of that. Show some respect to yourself. Move on.

4. Engage in exercise

As you read the above heading you're either filled with a glow of self-satisfaction as you already exercise, or a sense of dread or guilt because you don't. Well I hope the following encourages you wherever you are on the exercise spectrum to understand the significant benefits to your mental health when you engage in activity.

Now, whatever you do, don't skip this section. I'm not here to sell you a gym membership or get you to run a marathon. But I am here to demonstrate how one of the best ways to show yourself some respect is to get your body active. So sit back and relax. I promise this isn't going to hurt. Honest.

Psychologists have found that one of the most productive techniques for encouraging a more positive outlook in life is exercise.

So why's it so important? Well, to answer that, let's go back to our past.

You'll remember earlier we explored the impact our evolutionary ancestors still have on how we think and behave now. Our bodies have evolved to cope with anything causing tension and anxiety through a fight-or-flight response. Now as you'd expect, fight or flight is a physical response. And the body gears up for this physical response by releasing hormones, glucose and fats into the bloodstream.

But here's the really important point:

Without exercise they remain there.

It's the equivalent of eating several energy bars before a long hike and then deciding to slob at home watching television instead. The bars had a purpose – to give you some energy – but then you failed to burn it off. That has consequences, especially when done on a consistent basis.

Likewise adrenaline and cortisol in your body is fine in the short term. But it's present in anticipation of some fighting or fleeing. When there is no physical activity it then disrupts your body's natural balance and you can become agitated and anxious.

So the anxious mood you find yourself in could be blamed on your circumstances, when in fact it's simply reflecting how you feel given the chemicals and hormones currently in your bloodstream.

With me so far? Good.

Another way in which we can feel good through exercise is when we've made love, or have been involved in some physical intimacy lasting longer than five minutes. Such activity releases a hormone called oxytocin, sometimes referred to as the love hormone. Oxytocin evokes feelings of contentment, reductions in anxiety, and feelings of calmness and security around a mate. (See, I told you it would be worth reading this section didn't I?) So although you might not feel in the mood for some lovemaking and intimacy, it could be precisely what you need to help you relax and calm yourself down.

Now obviously dealing with your problems and hopefully resolving them will help you feel better, but exercise will also have the same effect on your mind – even if your problem persists.

In fact, the case for doing some form of exercise is overwhelming. Here are a few benefits.

Ready?

- It can improve your mental functioning by increasing blood circulation to the brain. You may have heard the phrase 'exercise clears my head.' Well, actually it does. You will often feel mentally sharper as a result of exercise. The likelihood is that you'll think with a greater clarity and perhaps see a solution to an issue after some physical activity that you hadn't seen before.

- Exercise can calm you down. It releases the brain's natural opiates, endorphins, which produce a calmer, happier state. Personally I cannot think of a better antidote when you're feeling stressed or anxious. Exercise is literally putting you in the right state to deal with your challenges.

- Another positive benefit that is often overlooked is the impact exercise has on our feeling of self-mastery and self-discipline. We're taking responsibility for our health, we're being proactive rather than passive about our lifestyle. This makes us feel good about ourselves, raises our self-esteem and reduces the impact of negative emotions.

- The physical act of lovemaking can strengthen the bond and sense of trust between two people through the release of the hormone we looked at earlier, oxytocin. Not a bad state to be in if you're facing some difficulties.

Quite an impressive list, wouldn't you say?

I experience an overwhelming sense of personal satisfaction when I know I've had a good physical workout. And I also know how I feel when days have turned into weeks without me expending any physical energy. Lethargy creeps in, as do pangs of guilt. Not exactly the best cocktail of emotions to be experiencing when I then find myself faced with a particular challenge.

Dr Raj Persaud, a former consultant psychologist at the Maudsley Hospital in London and Honorary Senior Lecturer at the Institute of Psychiatry, clearly sees the benefits of exercise for our mental health. He writes:

> *'If you want to stay sane in this increasingly stressful world, regular exercise can be as effective, if not more so, than a weekly appointment with a therapist.'*
> (*Staying Sane – How to make your mind work for you*,
> Bantam Books, 2001, p. 336.)

He indicates that over a thousand scientific studies on exercise have shown it holds remarkable benefits for our mental health.

Remarkable benefits?

And yet some people come up with a whole host of what are sometimes rather lame excuses for avoiding it. The quick fix of a pill seems to be more appealing to some people than the thought of actually doing something for themselves to improve their mood. You know what? Such an approach is again showing disrespect for ourselves.

So if you already exercise I hope you're even more convinced of its benefits. And if you don't, perhaps it's time to do a reality check.

Logic screams at us that a crucial strategy in helping us live with less worry, anxiety and stress would be more physical activity. But there's a problem. Logic rarely motivates. So what may help? Well, let's start by first dealing with a couple of objections for why people don't exercise.

1. I don't have time

First let's be honest and admit that we always find time for what we really want to do. If it's important we make the time. To the question 'Why don't you exercise?' the more honest answer actually would be to say 'I've chosen not to make it a priority at the moment.' At least that way you're talking as someone who sounds like they're in charge of their life rather than a victim of circumstances.

So is a lack of time an easy excuse or a genuine reason?

If it's a genuine reason, think about the following. Remember when we looked earlier at the circle of concern and circle of influence? Well, this would be a great time to focus on your circle of influence in terms of the amount of physical activity you take. We can all be 'time challenged' on occasions, but I'm not suggesting we have to find two extra hours a day six days of the week. Thirty minutes of physical activity incorporated daily into your week should do the trick. From taking the stairs more often, walking to places and maybe even going on a bike ride, it all adds up. Hey, you may even think about ballroom dancing, as one of my clients did recently. They love it and they're meeting new people.

And if you're currently smiling to yourself and thinking 'there's no way anyone is ever going to get me to change my lifestyle', that ultimately is your choice. It's your life. I won't be offended. It's your call.

But remember, you're the one who's reading this book.

My guess is the subject matter must be of some interest and relevance. And I'm pointing out a great way to enjoy life more and worry a lot less. No offence, but unless you're physically incapacitated in some way I reckon you'd be rather silly to ignore it. Actually I think silly is being a little too kind. You get my point.

2. I detest gyms

Well, you're not alone. But why equate physical activity with gyms? Any form of exercise can benefit you. Your goal is to find something you enjoy. I do enjoy the gym, but I also love to go on long walks near where I live. My son enjoys playing squash, my wife runs with a group of friends, and my daughter dances. None of us do so with the primary aim of combating stress, we do it because we enjoy doing it. That's the key. You must enjoy it, to some degree anyway.

I recently recommended walking as an activity to a client of mine. I knew it would benefit him both physically and mentally. He gave up after three days.

Shame.

But then he bought a puppy.

Not only has the dog been a welcome distraction, but he now feels he has no choice but to go out for a walk at least twice a day. Interestingly, that only adds up to around forty minutes a day. But when you add that up over a year it equates to over 240 hours. Now if we say that people in employment work an average of 37 hours per week that means my client spends approximately six and a half weeks a year walking his dog. You see, even a moderate amount of exercise adds up over time. So perhaps it's time to ditch the excuses and start searching for solutions. After all, you wouldn't dream of keeping your thoroughbred horse locked up inside a stable, would you? You'd make sure it gets sufficient exercise.

It would be cruel not to.

Agree?

Good.

Now it's over to you.

Hammock time — for those who currently exercise

- If you do take exercise estimate how many hours that adds up to in a week. Your aim should be at least 3 hours (If you have a physically demanding job or you care for small children you may find you get sufficient exercise anyway).

- Is the above figure based on what you intend to do each week or actually do?
- What strategies do you use in order to create time to exercise?
- Aside from injury or ill health is there anything else that hinders you taking as much exercise as you'd like?
- Recognizing the range of benefits you gain from exercise, what do you need to be aware of in order to maintain or perhaps even increase the amount you take each week?

Hammock time — for those who don't currently exercise sufficiently

- List the two main reasons why you don't take sufficient exercise each week. (If there are health reasons then please consult with a doctor before beginning any exercise programme.)
- Given your answers to the above question, would you say your answers are genuine reasons or rather poor excuses?
- Now identify something that you do enjoy doing physically. (You may not have done it for years – maybe not since you were at school – but you do enjoy it.)
- What are the reasons you no longer do it?
- How realistic would it be to start doing that activity again?

- What other physical activity could you start to incorporate into your life? (Remember, don't be overambitious. Start small. Be realistic. You want to attempt something that is achievable.)
- Identify a person who could help you or be your cheerleader. (My wife finds running with a couple of friends or going to an exercise class with my daughter far more motivating than doing so alone.)
- If you were to take one single action today towards increasing your physical activity, what would it be?

Right, so in terms of showing some respect to yourself we've looked at starting to change your scripts, avoiding going it alone, letting go of grudges and engaging in exercise. Now for our fifth and final strategy.

5. Postpone permanently pleasing people

A key reason why people worry is around their relationships with others. Wanting to avoid conflict is understandable. But do we sometimes go too far in our desire to keep others happy?

Why is that?

As we were growing up we were conditioned to behave in a particular way. When we lived up to these pre-set standards determined by our parents (or whoever else was bringing us up) we were generally rewarded. This may have simply been through verbal praise like 'Good boy,' or 'That's a good girl' or with something tangible like some sweets or other treat. In some sad cases our reward was simply the avoidance of punishment.

Equally, if we failed to conform to expectations, rewards were withdrawn or threats were possibly made. The classic example for many families would have been 'If you're not good I'll tell Father Christmas and he won't bring you any presents.' (I have to confess that this particular threat made by my own mum was something I gradually tired of and became quite complacent about as I reached my mid-thirties.)

So in a nutshell, we've become conditioned to believe that when you please other people rewards or expressions of love follow and if you don't conform they'll be withdrawn. To be fair, as a way of getting young children with still undeveloped brains to behave it's a pretty decent strategy.

However, as we get older the legacy of such conditioning for some of us is that in order to be accepted we must continue to embark on a daily mission of pleasing people.

All the time.

Every day.

Forever.

And when we don't, we believe we risk rejection. We may even risk a mild form of persecution in the form of criticism from others. If you're like my mate Dave this is no big deal. He's fairly self-contained, full of self-belief and remains unfazed by what others think of him, except perhaps very close family.

But we're not all like Dave.

Maybe you're a little more like me.

Or should I say a little like how I used to be.

You see, based on a whole list of reasons, some complex and some straightforward, I unconsciously embarked upon a quest to permanently please people.

The very thought of criticism or rejection would cause me to inwardly recoil and squirm with discomfort. Therefore I continually worried about what others thought of me.

I analyzed my encounters with others.

I replayed conversations over and over in my mind.

I second guessed what others thought of me.

When I tried on new clothes my first question was not 'do I like it?' but 'What will others think?'

I once chose the colour of a car based on the fact that my mum would like it. (Pink always was her favourite colour.)

But seriously, let me tell you that such an approach to life is not a recipe for fun, freedom and self-fulfilment. Quite simply, I had fallen into the trap of living life based on what others think of me rather than on what I'd like to do.

Big mistake.

With hindsight I realize the underlying reasons for my behaviour. I think most people, if they're honest, want to be liked an accepted. In fact our evolutionary ancestors knew that being accepted by their tribe was key to their survival. Rejection for whatever reason would result in limited life opportunities.

Or to be more blunt, death.

Even my friend Dave, beneath his rugged, manly Yorkshire countenance, wants to be liked. He really does. But if you don't like him that's your loss.

Not his.

That's the difference between him and a whole host of other people. He stresses a lot less, if at all, about what others think of him.

And although I'll never completely embrace Dave's outlook on life, I do recognize that I can learn from him. If I want to enjoy life more and worry a lot less then he's a half-decent role model. He knows that learning to please others is a necessity and a great way to get on in life. But it's not an obsession. He's not a prisoner to other people's perceptions. Intuitively he's bought into an insight from the American actor Bill Cosby, who often quoted to have said:

> *'I'm not sure of the definition of success. But I know the definition of failure. Trying to please everybody all of the time.'*

Unconscious beliefs that underpin our desire to please people include:

> *I must always be perfect.*
>
> *Acceptance by others must be my constant goal.*
>
> *Acceptance by others means I'm an OK person.*
>
> *Rejection and criticism must be avoided at all costs.*

The real truth is this is completely unrealistic. Period.

And yet our obsession about what others think of us can be taken to extremes. I heard recently about the great musical composer Edward Elgar, who was photographed on his death bed before he died, so concerned was he about his image! But are we ourselves in danger of becoming a little too obsessed with our image, our performance and what others think of us? Am I failing to find my voice and make my mark in life because I'm too concerned about being misconstrued or misunderstood? Am I playing safe and playing small because I don't want to risk upsetting others?

And is this underlying tension between who I really am and the person I'm pretending to be part of the reason for my underlying anxiety?

Challenging stuff, eh?

Maybe it's time to let go of the unrealistic expectation you place on yourself and your desire to please others, and buy into a new set of beliefs, which may include:

- I make mistakes but I'm still an OK person

- I'm learning and developing every day

- I value my progress, not perfection

- It's great to please others, but it's not the only reason I'm on this planet

- My criteria for success is not based solely on what others think of me

- I recognize and respect the many qualities I have

- I fully accept I'm on a journey and I'm not there yet

- I'm like the Leaning Tower of Pisa. My flaws make me unique

Eight positive and realistic beliefs for you to buy into as a person. By doing so you help relieve some of the pressure you might be placing yourself under that is generated by a potentially extreme desire to please others.

Hammock time

If you had to choose three of the above beliefs that you want to adopt which would they be? Or perhaps you'd prefer to come up with three of your own. Either way, write them down.

1.
2.
3.

Now be aware this is not an invitation to abandon decent behaviour and adopt a 'Sod them, couldn't care less' attitude to people. But it is a challenge to question for whose benefit you're living your life.

Perhaps we have something to learn from the actor, writer and comedian Ricky Gervais, who in an interview with the *Guardian* (4 November 2011) said; 'When I first came into [showbusiness] I was very conscious of reputation. I thought it was everything. And now I think, no, it's not actually. Because reputation is what strangers think you're like. Character is what you're really like. And all my best friends and family know what my character is.'

So show some respect to yourself and be more realistic about your ability to please others. And make sure you reread that Bill Cosby quote. It could save you a lot of stress and worry when you recognize its truth.

In a nutshell

Show a little respect to yourself, reduce your worries and increase your enjoyment of life:

- Start changing your scripts – be more aware of the conversations you have with yourself.
- Avoid going it alone – seek support and advice from others.
- Let go of grudges – you decide if you become bitter or better.
- Engage in exercise – unless you're physically unable you'd be silly not to.
- Postpone permanently pleasing people – you're never going to please everyone all of the time – and that's OK.

Chapter 8

How to Make Your Environment Friendly

So far in this 'Move On' section we've looked at 'Let's Get Rational' and how to use your rational brain to tackle your worries. We've hopefully had some fun as we've learnt how to manage our imagination and we've just looked at five ways to show some respect to ourselves. In this last section let's explore some more practical ways in which to worry less and enjoy life more.

I learnt about osmosis at school. Biology was never my favourite subject, but I learnt that by an automatic process plants absorb water from their environment.

Our environment can have a similar effect on us. What surrounds us affects us. And it's not always to our benefit. You see, there can be a build-up of environmental poisons that weakens our emotional immune system, but which develops gradually and often subtly. And because it's gradual and subtle we might not even notice the impact our environment is having on us.

An illustration you may have come across before reinforces the point further.

It's often referred to as the boiled frog syndrome. If you've not come across this before you'll find it fascinating. Let me explain.

Apparently if you place a live frog in a pan of boiling water it jumps out immediately. I guess that's no surprise. However, if you place a frog in a pan of lukewarm water (you can probably use the same frog if you wish) it will swim around quite happily.

Now this next bit is interesting.

If you then gradually heat the water up slowly over time it is possible for the temperature of the water to reach boiling point before the frog (by which time it's too late) realizes it's being boiled alive.

In other words, the frog's death (at least in this illustration) is caused by the gradual rather than the dramatic change in its environment.

Interesting, eh?

The frog didn't realize its changing environment was slowly leading to its death.

A fairly dramatic illustration, I appreciate, and not an experiment I'm suggesting you try at home with the children, or with anyone else for that matter.

Now clearly I'm not suggesting that we're living in the equivalent of a pan of boiling water. But I am suggesting that sometimes our environment is unhealthy and the consistent and gradual exposure to certain factors does little to help our stress levels. But because these factors are often subtle and go unnoticed we fail to appreciate their impact on us.

So what does our problem boil down to? (Sorry for the pun.)

Awareness.

Or should I say a lack of awareness on our part.

But can I be blunt for a moment?

A lack of awareness is no excuse. Ignorance is not our escape route. Just ask that frog. The reality is our environment could be contributing to our anxiety and stress levels, and impacting our enjoyment of life, whether we're aware of it or not. So in this chapter we're going to explore five ways we can make our environment friendly, keep that pan of water at a safe temperature and avoid creating a climate where our worries flourish.

So let's get started with our first one.

1. Manage your mental diet

What we feed our bodies can potentially make us sick. If you've ever eaten or drunk too much you'll know what I mean.

Sickness can happen quickly.

However, the long-term after-effects of an unhealthy diet can take years to manifest. But either way, the reality is that what we consume can make us unwell.

Likewise, what we allow our minds to consume can also affect our emotional wellbeing. Sometimes this can be healthy, stimulating and uplifting. Other times, less so.

The real truth is this:

> When we allow the airwaves
> and atmosphere of our environment
> to be filled with negativity,
> it has consequences

Now I'm not suggesting that watching two hours of news makes you sick. Nor am I saying that a daily consumption of negative news is the sole cause of your worries and anxieties.

But I am saying that it could be a contributory factor, especially if your mental diet is unbalanced.

You see, some health issues are not simply down to what we eat but also to what we don't eat. What we lack in our diet can have a detrimental effect on us, which is why we're encouraged to eat more fruit and vegetables (and preferably not as a side order to your double cheeseburger, fizzy drink and fries).

And from a mental wellbeing perspective it is possible to consume information that is lacking in any kind of inspiration or positivity.

Now hear me right. This is not a call to abandon the daily news and only devour self-help books and inspirational videos on YouTube. Neither am I suggesting a total news blackout (although you might want to try it for a week and see how it feels).

I'm suggesting some balance.

Perhaps you need to decide consciously the amount of news you read or listen to. Maybe your consumption of it needs to be the equivalent of having a light lunch rather than a state banquet. And perhaps it's time for you to look for information and ideas that feed your soul rather than pollute it. Pump enough poison into a river and the fish die. Pump enough negativity, doom and gloom into your head and physically you won't die.

But neither will you thrive.

And inspiration shouldn't be confused with motivation.

The word 'inspire' simply means 'to breathe life into'. Watching a comedian can breathe life into you. Being engaged in a hobby or interest can do the same. Some television is both moving and profound. Movies can be also. And there are a number of news programmes that can be informative and inspiring.

So by all means keep your feet on the ground and stay in touch with reality, but keep your head up and your eyes open to the many amazing things this world contains.

Seek out stuff that feeds you, not bleeds you.

Don't allow the promotion of problems through the media to draw a curtain over your mind to the potential and possibilities that are also part of the picture.

Here's the real truth:

> What you focus on magnifies

So remember, news is not the norm. That's why it's news. But consume enough of it and it will soon seem that way. And if we're not careful our perception of the world, no matter how limited or edited, will become our reality.

That's far from inspiring when you're looking through a biased news lens that focuses on a certain part of the picture without letting you see the whole landscape.

So be aware, and perhaps even be wary when consuming the news. And be more conscious of what type of information you're downloading into your mind.

Hammock time

- On a daily basis how much news do you consume?
- What's the first thing you listen to or read when you wake up in a morning?
- What's the last thing you listen to or read before you go to sleep?
- On reflection, is there something you could consume at the start and end of your day that would be more beneficial than what you're currently doing?
- If so, what would it be?
- What specifically breathes life into you and causes you to feel better about life?
- Is there a need to increase the amount of 'soul food' you consume? (By 'soul food' I mean activities that breathe life into you.)

However, please be aware that our mental diet is not solely influenced by what we read, watch or listen to, but also by the people we hang around with. So in terms of developing an environment that nourishes your wellbeing you need to be careful about the people you hang around with. That's why this next section is so important to creating a friendlier environment.

2. Escape from escalators

There's a phrase or saying you may be familiar with that states 'a trouble shared is a trouble halved'. And in my experience that can indeed be the case. But I would add an important caveat to that phrase.

'A trouble shared *with the right person* is a trouble halved.'

You see, in my experience a trouble shared with the *wrong person* can make the trouble doubled.

I call these kind of people 'Escalators'. They have the ability to escalate your problem and by doing so add fuel to your worries.

Typically Escalators like to binge on bad news and then feel it's their duty to help spread a little misery amongst everyone they know. Their mission statement would read 'Make mountains out of molehills'. Positive news is viewed with suspicion and scepticism in the same way you might view some unusual food you've never tried before.

Let's listen to an Escalator in conversation:

You: *I had a better month in business than I was expecting but I'm still a little concerned about the future.*

Escalator: *You've every right to be. I was watching the news last night and they think things are going to get worse.*

You: *Really? I didn't see that.*

Escalator: *You can probably still see it on iPlayer. Looks like this could be the worst economic crisis since the great depression in the 1920s.*

You: *Well I guess I must be fortunate then. Like I say, we've had a good month.*

Escalator: *That was probably just a one off. You need to look at the long-term future. I don't think we'll ever get back to how things were. It's going to affect everyone. But it's the young people I feel sorry for. What have they got to look forward to?*

You get my point? Their ability to escalate an issue in turn sees your own morale fall.

Now, when you're in a reasonably secure and stable frame of mind, Escalators can almost be seen as mildly amusing. Their woeful insights regarding the world can be easily batted away by you without too much effort.

But when you're struggling emotionally, when your anxieties have weakened you, then suddenly it's as if your bat has been coated with glue. And when an Escalator bowls you another ball of negativity it's harder to hit away. Their views of life, fuelled perhaps by their own worries and concerns, stick to you. And some Escalators have more than one ball to bowl. Give them enough airtime and they'll be quick to seize the moment.

Now, to be fair to Escalators, their behaviour rarely stems from malicious intent. Like the rest of us they're very often operating on autopilot without thinking consciously about what they're saying. I'm sure many of them would be horrified if they realized the impact their behaviour was having on others. And Escalators, after all, are only expressing how they in fact see the world. It might be a distorted picture, but to them it's their reality.

Escalators of course may have a point to a degree – I'm not suggesting they're lying. But the word 'hope' rarely appears in their vocabulary and they can provide you with a biased and distorted view of life. And in doing so they can magnify your own concerns and anxieties.

Take my word for it: if you're feeling vulnerable you do really need to be careful who you're spending time with.

So if you need to escape from Escalators, who do you turn to for support?

In my experience two particular traits are invaluable in finding help from others. First, the ability to listen well and, second, a solution-orientated focus.

You see, sometimes the opportunity to air your worries can be enough in itself to bring a sense of clarity and perspective. Simply talking through your problems and being listened to can be of enormous benefit. When more help is required, someone who is able to acknowledge the reality of your issue but then help you to seek possible solutions is invaluable. They're not denying the problem but they are helping you to explore ways of dealing with it.

So be aware of your environment in terms of who you spend time with. Recognize the people who help you and those that perhaps unwittingly drain you. And remember, just because an Escalator doesn't mean any harm doesn't excuse the fact that they might still be causing some.

Now, if you have an Escalator in your life, it's up to you to decide how best to deal with them. And to some extent that depends on how close your relationship is with them.

Clearly your escape from an Escalator is far easier when you have little or occasional contact with them.

A closer relationship, however, is perhaps more tricky to deal with. The key question to ask is: is the behaviour of the other person seriously impacting you or not? If you're aware of this trait and able to easily dismiss it, then fine. But if not, then perhaps rather than tell them to stop their behaviour, which may cause them to feel defensive, it's more helpful to express what you want them to start doing instead.

For instance, you might say, 'I'm feeling a little vulnerable and fragile at the moment. I'd really appreciate it if you could help keep my spirits up, help me remain positive and sometimes just listen to me, OK?'

In a close relationship this approach will really help. Remember, their escalating is not born out of malicious intent. And to further reinforce their positive behaviour, make sure you acknowledge it. For example, 'I've really appreciated your support over the last few days. It's meant a lot to me and you've helped me see the world is not all doom and gloom. Thank you.'

Hammock time

- Who are the people in your life who might be described at times as Escalators?
- How does their behaviour affect you?
- What approach, if any, do you currently take to deal with them? How could you deal with them in the future?
- Do you feel you yourself could sometimes fall into the category of an Escalator in terms of how you talk about your problems?
- Given the above, what do you need to do less of in future and what do you need to start doing more of instead?

- Identify the people who are good to be around. If you don't feel you have enough of them then perhaps you need to take action to widen your circle of friends.
- If that's the case, what one practical step could you take today to do so? (Perhaps something as simple as joining Facebook could be a start.)

OK, let's explore another area to create an environment that reduces our chances of experiencing worry, anxiety and stress.

3. Cut the clutter

Let's return to our earlier example of that thoroughbred horse. Not only is it fed well and exercised regularly, but it also needs warmth and shelter. You don't leave a thoroughbred out on the moors in freezing conditions or in a stable up to its knees in manure. If you did you'd be done for cruelty. The horse needs mucking out daily and the right environment in which to thrive.

And we're no different.

You're a rare person if you thrive in a chaotic, cluttered environment. It's not impossible to do so, but it's rare. And yet that's how some people live. Their stressors aren't so tangible, they're perhaps more subtle, but remember the boiled frog syndrome? That water's heating up and we're not even aware of it.

But like a tyre with a slow puncture, people's sense of peace and calm is slowly deflating when they live in an environment of continuous clutter.

So what's the way forward?

To a large extent that depends on your current domestic circumstances. I recognize we don't all have the luxury of living in the equivalent of some yoga retreat centre surrounded by perfumed candles and the sound of running water.

Some of us may have young children as part of our environment. Now I'm not suggesting children are clutter, but they can be a great source of it. One point to recognize, though, is that the number of toys you give them is not in direct correlation to the amount of love you have for them. Fewer toys do not mean less love. But it will mean less clutter and more space.

Whether we have children or not, we probably also need to wake up to the fact that so much of what most of us own is no longer needed or necessary.

Having moved house recently, I realized that at least a quarter of what we owned was surplus to requirements. And by clearing out what was no longer required, I became aware of what we did need but had forgotten we even had (which included a long-forgotten relative and an old lawn mower).

In doing so I realized that too much stuff can clutter your mind. And when there's too much clutter in our lives we lack clarity in our thinking. And just as confusion can stem from a cluttered mind, a cluttered home or workspace can impair your ability to think and act straight. In other words, your environment is subtly affecting how you're thinking and feeling.

OK, so what am I saying? Tidy up where you live and work, and you can kiss goodbye to your worries from now on?

Of course not.

But we do increase our anxiety and perpetuate our stress when we feel we have no control – or feel we're losing control.

Here's the real truth:

> Taking charge of your environment and making realistic changes, no matter how small, can increase your sense of control and personal wellbeing

Now you might feel inspired to undertake a mass clear-out and, trust me, you will feel better for doing so, but even small changes can make a difference. And if you feel overawed by the potential scale of the task, take heart.

First, you haven't seen my daughter's bedroom. That alone should put the scale of your clutter into perspective. Second, start small. Your goal is not to declutter your whole house over-night. That task is too large.

How about you simply set aside seven minutes. Yep, that's right, just seven minutes. What can be achieved in such a short space of time? Well, probably not a lot, but that's not the point. The real truth is this:

> Starting a potentially unpleasant task is always harder than actually continuing it

If you only do seven minutes that's fine. You won't feel a failure – after all, that was your target. But my guess is once you've got started you'll want to carry on for longer. Momentum fuels motivation. Achieving some success in your decluttering journey will make you feel better about yourself.

Be careful to focus on progress, not perfection. Celebrate small wins. And as you do, your sense of ownership of the problem and personal pride in tackling it will increase.

It almost sounds too simple and straightforward, doesn't it? But why seek complex solutions when none are required?

Hammock time

So are you the king or queen of clutter? If not, great. You're already doing something that plays a part in helping you reduce your environmental stressors. But if you are, then consider these next questions:

- Which area of your life needs de-cluttering as a priority – your work or your home life?
- Identify a room or area you need to de-clutter.
- Set aside 7 minutes to start de-cluttering sometime in the next 24 hours.
- Apart from the sense of satisfaction from starting the task, what little reward will you give yourself when the task is complete?

Here's one idea I've started to use. I focus now more on the quality of my clothing than the quantity. So, when moving house recently, I eased my emotional loss of giving away some shirts to a charity with the reward of treating myself to a really smart new one. My wardrobe looks less cluttered as a result and the stress of not being able to find things has been significantly reduced.

So far we've explored the need to manage your mental diet, escape from Escalators and cut the clutter. Let's look at our remaining strategies that could help you worry less and enjoy life more.

4. Find the funny

The Book of Proverbs states that laughter is good medicine. It would seem that scientists also agree with this ancient wisdom. Scientists at Waterloo University in Ontario, Canada established that exposure to humour improves immune system functioning, producing significant rises in the body's natural defences such as antibodies in the bloodstream. But despite this good news about the benefits of humour I realize that, when you're worried and anxious about a particular issue, being encouraged to look for the funny may seem both patronizing and unrealistic.

I've got some empathy for that viewpoint.

Clearly there are some scenarios where such advice could border on the offensive. So please bear with me. This is a possible strategy that *in certain cases* will help you see things in perspective and maintain your morale in difficult circumstances.

Let me elaborate.

As I have mentioned in previous chapters, during the writing of this book I went into hospital for a routine operation. It only required a local anaesthetic and, whilst I was advised to avoid any physical activity for a week or so, I was told I would soon be back to normal. And so for the next few days packets of painkillers and some frozen peas became my constant companions. However, whilst the swelling went down, thanks in part I'm sure to me religiously using the frozen peas (which did cause a mixture of mild concern and amusement when out shopping or visiting friends), the pain on the other hand stubbornly refused to leave. In fact, it seemed to worsen on some days. Maintaining a positive attitude in the face of such discomfort wasn't easy.

Days dragged into weeks and concerns grew for how long my pain would last. The temptation was to research on the internet whether other people had had such problems. But I was loath to do so.

I saw this as a way of potentially feeding my fears. Internet forums were unlikely to be filled with messages from people who'd experienced no problems. Why would they be? If you've not experienced any problems, why go online to read about people who have, unless you're rather sad and there's nothing on television.

Therefore I reasoned that whatever I read was bound to give a distorted and sometimes biased view of my current challenges. To put it bluntly, if you're feeling depressed it probably does little long-term good to speak to other depressed people.

The other significant challenge I faced was my business, which relies heavily on my own personal input. An unwell Paul McGee is bad for business, when my main source of income comes from me speaking at events and coaching clients.

My circumstances could well have been described under the headline 'Worrying times', which would have been somewhat ironic considering I was writing a book called *How Not to Worry*.

But I guess I had a choice.

Be weighed down by the worry or work through it.

I saw humour as one of my strategies to help me deal with my situation. It was a conscious decision on my part.

My good friend Richard texted me to see how I was health-wise. Here's an extract from my reply:

> *'To be honest mate I'm not doing well. Probably sound like a martyr I know, but I'm finding things really difficult. In constant pain/ discomfort and tired out by it all. It's hard work putting on a brave face and carrying on as normal. When we chat I might prefer not to talk about it 1) cos I don't want to sound like a moaner and 2) in my low moments I actually get a little emotional.'*

Now it's the next part of my reply that I want to highlight.

> *'So humour and frivolity are the order of the day.'*

Richard's reply was perfect. And included the following lines:

> *'Toothache of the testicles cannot be easy to live with! So fun and frivolity is the order of the day – no problem... just as long as you don't mistake it for not caring.'*

He then proceeded to tell me a joke. It was the perfect tonic. My physical pain and discomfort remained, but in one text Richard had lifted my spirits. Realizing the impact his text message had on me made me realize that, like many challenges in life, the battle is often not just physical but mental also. I knew finding the funny was an important weapon in my arsenal.

Weeks later I now find myself almost completely free of any discomfort. I'm not naïve enough to suggest that humour was the key to my recovery – time was undoubtedly a large factor, plus the body's own healing mechanism, but I genuinely believe humour helped the healing process.

Hammock time

- Without trivializing your situation, what steps could you take to help you 'find the funny'?
- Who is the person you know who could bring some humour into your life?
- What other ways could help you find the funny? (YouTube could be a great place to start and there will be thousands of sites on the internet that could help bring some humour into your life.)

Finding the funny might not seem the most natural response to combat worry and stress, but by making your environment friendlier in this way it can be another way to feed your soul. Be more conscious of its impact and appreciate that humour can bring you a sense of perspective that puts you in a better frame of mind to tackle your challenges.

Right, that's four ways we explored on how to make your environment friendly. Let's look now at the final one.

5. Muse to the music

Sounds influence how you feel. And not always in a positive way. I've had plenty of experiences where the banging created by builders becomes not just distracting and annoying but can be quite distressing. And if you've ever been on a plane with a screaming child you'll know the impact sound can have on your stress levels, particularly when it's a long-haul flight.

From mild irritation to intense frustration, sounds can definitely impact your mood, especially when they're persistent.

So in order to make your environment friendly, become more aware of the sounds that fill the air. Is it a blaring television, loud rock music, or something a little more relaxing?

Clearly, listening to music you enjoy has a positive impact on your sense of wellbeing. Obviously. But do we always appreciate this fact? Are we conscious of the music we listen to in our home, or in our car? Because rock may be your favourite kind of music but, when you're stuck in rush-hour traffic with little sign of getting anywhere quickly, is what you're listening to revving up your mood or relaxing you? If you're pumping up the volume you might also be pumping up the tension.

Now this section of the book is not being sponsored by the classical music appreciation society. However, there are types of music that are more calming than others, and they typically fall within the classical category. So you might want to chill out with some Chopin, bask in some Beethoven and savour some Schubert.

In fact, such music could form part of your mental diet that we explored earlier.

As I write these words now I have some classical music playing in the background. I've no idea what it is and I struggle to tell the difference between Elgar and Mozart, but I am aware of the impact it has on my mood. And I do find it particularly relaxing when I'm driving. It's fair to say I've seen classical music in the past as something old people are into. Well, I guess to some people I now fall into that category. The point is, I've not always been a fan of this type of music, and maybe you're not either. But how about you introduce a little into your life? You never know, it might even grow on you.

And if it doesn't, fine. Just remember that music impacts your mood and if you're feeling all stressed up with no one to choke then the right tune could do just enough to relax you a little.

In a nutshell

Our environment can have a gradual and some-times subtle long-term impact on us. So:

1 Manage your mental diet – be careful what messages you're filling your mind with.
2 Escape from Escalators – be careful who you hang around with and who you share your problems with.
3 Cut the clutter – clutter creates confusion and counteracts calm. Reduce it. In the next 24 hours.
4 Find the funny – laughter really is the best medicine.
5 Muse to the music – music affects your mood so be careful what you choose to listen to.

And Finally...

Well, we're nearly at the end of our journey together. (Well, in terms of looking at the subject of worry anyway – who knows if we'll bump into each other in the future.)

We've looked at why worry is such a big deal despite the fact that we're wealthier and healthier than we've ever been. We've taken some time to explore why we worry, ranging from perhaps the surprising fact that we actually enjoy it right through to the fact that we're actually wired to do so.

We've also discovered there's a key difference between 'worth it worry', which can motivate us to take action and address our concerns and challenges, and 'worthless worry', which can trigger anxiety and stress and rob us of enjoying a more fulfilled and fruitful life.

We have found that fear can be both our friend and foe, and that without it there probably wouldn't be much chance of the human race actually surviving.

We've also lifted the lid on how our brain has developed and the relationship between primitive, emotional and rational brain. In doing so we've discovered how and why being rational can be so difficult at times.

We've explored how we can get lost in loopy logic, including the fact that we actually often feed our own fears, sometimes play the victim role and decide to wear worry as an identity. We've also slain the myth that positive happy thinking is the best weapon to banish our worries and how such an approach can in some cases actually make things a whole lot worse. It can also be a subtle form of avoidance and denial.

Having done some stopping and understanding in the first part of the book, we moved on to explore some solutions.

Although primitive and emotional brain have the bragging rights in terms of age and influence, we've discovered two very practical ways to maximize our rational brain, developing a Triple A strategy of awareness, analysis and action through to increasing our influence.

Then we focused on what perhaps some people may consider to be the slightly more creative or maybe, if you're so inclined, wacky approach to managing your imagination. We've explored some exercises that you may or may not have ever considered doing before but which from personal experience I have found can help you weaken your worries and address your anxieties. As a result we may all now have more friends than we did at the start of the book – even if some of them have long since departed the planet.

In Chapter 7, 'Show a Little Respect … to Yourself', we've been challenged to consider how we treat ourselves compared to how we'd look after a thoroughbred horse. To do so has meant we might need to change our scripts, i.e. the internal thoughts and conversations we have about ourselves and our situations. We also need to avoid going it alone and remember why depriving ourselves of support is like depriving ourselves of oxygen.

Couple that with letting go of grudges and engaging in exercise (including lovemaking), and you're well on the way to showing yourself some respect. Finally, add the fact that we need to postpone permanently pleasing people and you've embraced a whole host of ideas that will actually help you reduce your worry habit.

Our pervious chapter was all about making your environment friendly, and lessons we can learn from what happens when you place a frog in lukewarm water but gradually turn up the heat. As our summary of that chapter was only a couple of pages ago I'll trust you to remember why we might need to escape escalators, cut the clutter and find the funny.

So what's next?

In many ways that's for you to decide. There's plenty more that could be written on the subject, but there comes a time when the key to worrying less and enjoying life more is about implementation, not more information.

You might find it helpful to do a quick review of the book and highlight just three simple actions and changes you want to make. Ultimately there is no land called 'Total peace and tranquillity', but neither does your life experience have to be summed up with the words 'constant worry, stress and anxiety'.

The real truth is:

You can do something about your future

You will need support along the way, but ultimately it's the actions you now take that can lead to you enjoying life more.

Great, eh?

Well, actually that's a little scary to some people.

Even challenging, perhaps.

So start small. Start with the molehill, then build the mountain. I'm not suggesting a complete overhaul of your life. Just some small but noticeable changes. But small actions add up over time. You just need to begin. You see, whatever mistakes or issues you've had on your journey so far, there is a way forward.

Promise.

Take heart from these words from Maria Robinson. Read them more than once. Type them up if you have to:

'Nobody can go back and start a new beginning, but anyone can start today and make a new ending.'

Notice the words 'start today'. What could you do today to help yourself and perhaps others create a better way forward?

And focus on what you do want rather than what you don't want. It's time to change the script 'I wish I was less of a worrier' or 'I wish I wasn't such a stresshead' and start talking about what you do want and do enjoy instead. Perhaps the following question will help bring clarity to your thinking:

'What would you like to do, if you were less of a worrier?'

Go on, give that some thought, because it's the answer to that questions that will inspire you to take action.

And perhaps as you move forward spend a little less time focusing on your own needs and issues, and a little more time seeking to help others. Give self-focus a break from time to time.

It will do you good.

Honest.

And please take time to appreciate the following words from Dan Gardner, author of *Risk – The Science and Politics of Fear*, Virgin Books, 2008:

> 'Whatever challenges we face, it remains indisputably true that those living in the developed world are the safest, healthiest and richest humans who ever lived. We are still mortal. Sometimes we should worry [...], even be afraid. But we should always remember how very lucky we are to be alive now.'

OK? Good.

Well there you have it.

I'm moving on now to be the best imperfect person I can be.

Care to join me?

How Not to Worry... in a nutshell

If you're living in the developed world...

Your chances of living a longer, healthier, safer life are greater than any time in human history.

But despite this...

Worry, anxiety and stress are on the rise.

As humans we're the only animals that create stress with our own minds...

but here's some stuff to help you... and me.

1. There's rarely ever a perfect time or a perfect decision. Live with the imperfect. Including yourself.
2. Healthy fear can be a gift. As a species we owe our very existence to it.
3. Be careful of watching too much CNN... Constant Negative News.
4. Write stuff down. It declutters your mind.
5. Find the funny in stuff when you can. It will keep you sane.
6. Ask yourself 'Where is this issue on a scale of 1-10 (where 10 = death)?
7. If you can't control or influence it, learn to accept it.
8. Remember to re-tell is to re-live and that's not always helpful.
9. What you focus on magnifies. So be careful what you're focusing on.

10. Imagination is powerful. But if you're not enjoying the movies in your mind you can always shout 'cut'.

11. Depriving yourself of support is like depriving yourself of oxygen. Don't do it.

12. You can't start the next chapter of your life if you keep re-reading the last one. Move on.

Further Reading

Richard Carlson, *Don't Sweat the Small Stuff...*, Hodder Mobius, 2008.

Dale Carnegie, *How to Stop Worrying and Start Living*, Vermilion, 1998.

Charles H Elliot, Elaine Iljon Foreman and Laura L Smith, *Overcoming Anxiety for Dummies*, John Wiley and Sons, 2007.

Dr Raj Persaud, *Staying Sane – How to make your mind work for you*, Bantam Books, 2001.

Dr Martin Rossman, *The Worry Solution*, Rider, 2010.

Other titles from Paul McGee

Self Confidence: The Remarkable Truth of How a Small Change Can Make a Big Difference, 2nd edn, Capstone Publishing, 2012.

S.U.M.O. Shut Up, Move On: The Straight Talking Guide to Creating and Enjoying a Brilliant Life, 2nd edn, Capstone Publishing, 2011.

S.U.M.O. Your Relationships: How to Handle Not Strangle the People You Live and Work With, Capstone Publishing, 2007.

How to Write a CV that Really Works, How to Books, 2009.

Some helpful organizations

Depression Alliance
www.depressionalliance.org
0845 123 23 20
@DepressionAll

The Samaritans
www.samaritans.org
08457 90 90 90
@samaritans

S.A.D. (Seasonal Affective Disorder)
www.sad.org.uk

Citizens Advice Bureau
www.citizensadvice.org.uk
08444 111 444
@CitizensAdvice

Christians Against Poverty
www.capuk.org
01274 760720
@CAPuk

Consumer Credit Counselling Service
www.cccs.co.uk
0800 138 1111
@moneyaware

National Debt Line
www.nationaldebtline.co.uk
0808 808 4000
@natdebtline

Relate
www.relate.org.uk
0300 100 1234

Bring Paul McGee to your organization

Paul McGee speaks around the world at team events, conferences, workshops and retreats. From a one-hour keynote presentation to a three-day seminar, Paul tailors his material to your specific requirements, primarily in the areas of:

- Change

- Relationships

- Attitude

- Motivation

- Stress

- Confidence

- Leadership

- Customer Service

In order to make contact with Paul or learn more about SUMO4Schools

Email **Paul.McGee@the SumonGuy.com**

visit **www.TheSumoGuy.com**

or telephone **+44(0) 1925 268708**

Follow Paul on Twitter: **@TheSumoGuy**

Index

action
    imaginary 154–7
    increasing your influence
        130–43
    insights and reflections
        143, 144
    positive 99
    uncovering resources 129
analysis 122
    helpful 127–9
    historical 123
    hysterical 124–7
anticipatory stress 119, 153
anxiety
    be your own coach and
        challenger 126
    definition 15
    effect of imagination on
        146, 149–51, 157–8
    Escalators and 207–8
    memories and experiences
        52–5, 123
    new situations 37–9

    as normal 68
    see also stress; worry
attitude 46, 47, 137
avoidance behaviour 92–3
awareness
    after-effects of situation
        120–1
    current situation 118–19
    environmental 201
    future situation 119
    raising levels of 120, 121–2
    understanding and 26–8

bad news 55–60
beliefs 192–7
boiled frog syndrome 200–1
brain 75
    aware, accept, avoid 81
    emotional 77, 81–5, 100
    operating under pressure
        77–80
    primitive 69, 71–5, 77–80,
        85, 100

rational 77, 100
Buchholz, Todd 151

caring 46–8
Carnegie, Dale 129
challenge and pressure 24–5,
    37
change and uncertainty 36–7
circle of concern 130–1
clutter 210–14
comfort zone 38, 41, 105
conditioned behaviour 192–4
confirmation bias 91
control of situations 43–6,
    105, 132–8
Cosby, Bill 195, 197
Covey, Stephen R. 130
criticism, dealing with
    158–60, 194

Darwin, Charles 36
decision-making 103–7, 163
drama, need for 33–5
dreams 89

Einstein, Albert 151
Eisenberg, Larry 110
Elgar, Edward 196
emotions 77, 100
    effect of imagination on
        149
    engage rational brain 126

internal conversation
    170–1
keeping perspective 81–5
mental diet 202–5
rejection by a friend
    scenario 83–4
rumour and upbringing
    124–6
university student scenario
    81–3
environment
    awareness 201
    de-clutter 210–14
    escape from escalators
        205–10
    find the funny 214–17
    insights and reflections 219
    listen to music 218–19
    manage your mental diet
        202–5
    unhealthy 201
Escalators 206–10
exercise
    avoiding 187–90
    benefits 186–7
    effect of chemicals and
        hormones 185–6
    I detest gyms 189
    I don't have time 188–9
    importance 184–5
    insights and reflections
        190–2

fear
  acronyms 152
  complacency and 66–7
  constructive 67, 69–71
  effect of imagination on
    151–2
  excessive 68–9
  feeding 91–2
  fussing over 152–4
  irrational 88
  slugs example 71–5
  uncertainty and 105–6
fight-or-flight response 69,
  70–1, 74, 78, 185
Fogel, Robert 225
friends
  help with problem solving
    160–3
  imaginary conversations
    with 154, 159–61
  rejection by 83–4
fuzzy worry 140

game of life 26
Gervais, Ricky 197
grudges 180–4

happy thoughts 96–100, 127,
  138
humour 214–17
hysterical habit
  challenge your thinking 126

do the maths 126
primitive/emotional brain
  124
rumours and internet
  124–5
upbringing 125–6

identity 94–5
illusion of truth effect 58
imagination
  blessing and curse 151–2
  breakfast image 148
  controlling and harnessing
    154
  dealing with criticism
    158–60
  importance of 151–2
  insights and reflections
    165, 166
  making it work for you
    154–8
  mental movie example
    146–7
  PEAR process 148–51
  practical exercise 164–5
  problem solving with
    friends 160–3
  stress and fear 152–4
influence
  be proactive 130–1
  categories 131–3
  insights and reflections 143

personal 134–9
personal mantra 143
practical exercise 139–43
scale of 133–4
internal conversations 169–74

Journal of Personality and Social Psychology 138

knowledge and experience 37–42

labelling 94–5
Lagattula, Kristin 62–3
let go and move on 103
life expectancy 12–13
loopy logic
avoiding your issues 92–3
feeding your fears 91–2
giving power to 'things' and dates 100–2
how loopy can you be 110–13
just thinking happy thoughts 96–100, 127, 138
leads to loopy behaviour 90
paralysis by analysis 103–7
plane scenario 89–90
playing the victim role 93, 139

praying 108–10
rational thinking and 111
symptoms 91–107, 111–13
using worry as witchcraft 94
wearing worry as an identity 94–5, 129
worrying about the past 102–3

McGee, A. 110
media 55–60
mental wellbeing 12, 202–5, 217
Morewedge, Cary 89
mundane and routine 33–4
music 218–19

new job 39–42
Niebuhr, Reinhold 135
Norton, Michael 89

optimism 96–100

past events 102–3, 120
past experiences 52–5, 120, 123
P.E.A.R. process 148–51
perception of facts 45–6
Persaud, Raj 187
pleasing people 192–7
positive action 99

post-traumatic stress 120
prayer 108–10
pride 175–80
primitive brain 69, 85, 100
    act first think later 77–80
    actual/imagined events
        119–20
    slugs example 71–5
purpose in life 25

rational brain 77, 100
    loopy logic and 111–13
reasons
    challenge of change and
        uncertainty 36–7
    enjoy worrying 33–6
    gender differences 61–3
    identify main personal
        reasons 64
    insights and reflections
        42–3, 51–2, 60, 63–4
    lack of influence or control
        43–6
    lack of knowledge and
        experience 37–43
    overexposure to bad news
        55–9
    previous experiences 52–5
    unconscious aspect 30–2
    your upbringing 48–51
    your values 46–8
redundancy 135–7, 138–9

residual stress 120
    failure to seek support 120
    re-telling/re-living 121
respect *see* self-respect
responsibility 99, 101, 102
Rohn, Jim 97
role models 48–51
    imaginary conversations
        and actions 154–7
rumours 124–6

scale of influence 134–9
self-delusion 138
self-respect
    change your internal
        conversation 169–74
    engage in exercise 184–92
    insights and reflections
        198
    let go of grudges 180–4
    personal 168–9
    postpone permanently
        pleasing people 192–7
    seek support when needed
        175–80
Serenity Prayer 134–5
Shackleton, Ernest 154–5
stress
    anticipatory 119, 153
    being out of control 43–6
    being stupid 78
    definition 15

raising awareness 121–2

residual 120–1

seeking out 35

situational 119

types 119, 120

see also anxiety; worry

success and failure 42, 107,
150, 195, 197, 213

superstitions 100–2

support and advice 175–80

Triple A strategy

action 129

analysis 122–9

awareness 118–22

trouble shared is a trouble
halved 205–10

upbringing 48–52, 125–6

values 46–8

victim role 93, 139

Vincent-Peal, Norman 181

Von Restorff effect 58

Weil, Andrew 151–2

women as worriers 61–3

worry

dealing with 223–5

definition 15

helpful 127

historical 123

hysterical 124–7

impact 20–3, 63

insights and reflections
221–3, 226–7

meaning of 14–15

paper and elephant
example 46, 94

positive aspects 23–8

prevalence 12–14

terminology 20

Triple A strategy 118–29

using as witchcraft 94

wearing as an identity
94–5, 129

see also anxiety; stress

worry–stress–anxiety cycle
16, 18–19

barking dog example
16–18

(un)conscious level 19–20

worth it worry 15, 23, 68

worthless worry 15